Confucius

551 - 479 B.C.

Carpenter

Boston, April 6, 1985

Titles available in the Past Masters series:

CONFUCIUS

by Raymond Dawson

General Editor, Keith Thomas
PAST MASTERS SERIES

ᶿ Hill and Wang · New York
A division of Farrar, Straus and Giroux

Library of Congress Cataloging in Publication Data
Dawson, Raymond Stanley. Confucius.
(Past masters series) Bibliography: p. 91 Includes index.
1. Confucius I. Title. II. Series.
B128.C8D38 1982   181'.09512   82-12155
ISBN 0-8090-3596-0   ISBN 0-8090-1423-8 (pbk.)

Preface *and* Historical introduction

There are remarkably few books on Confucius in Western languages and fewer still which combine a high standard of scholarship with general readability. Indeed Arthur Waley's *The Analects of Confucius*, published in the thirties, is still essential reading. This little work is very different from anything else that has appeared. To the Western reader who knows nothing of Chinese civilisation the sayings of the Master may seem obscure or banal, so that the only way to appreciate them is to understand their formative influence on Chinese civilisation. In this book I am therefore as much concerned with the impact of the message as with the man himself. Since this involves some excursions into later Chinese history, I append a list of the major dynasties to help the reader to get his bearings. The names of some unfamiliar historical personages need to be mentioned, and these are dated and described in the index.

A preliminary sketch of China in Confucius's time is also necessary. It is impossible to bring his period into sharp focus since we have much less detailed information about life in fifth-century-BC China than is available concerning fifth-century-BC Athens. That city comes to life in the masterpieces of Euripides and Aristophanes, but there are no surviving works of literature to bear contemporary witness to life in Confucius's state of Lu. The age had no Herodotus or Thucydides to provide vivid accounts of the drama of war and politics.

The China of Confucius's lifetime was still nominally under the Chou Dynasty. The founders of that dynasty, Confucius's hero King Wen (the Cultured King), who paved the way, and his son King Wu (the Martial King), who made the actual conquest, had originally been satellites of the previous dynasty, the Shang. They came from the valley of the Wei, a tributary of the Yellow River, in the vicinity of present-day Sian. The Chou people cherished the tradition that they had conquered the Shang because that dynasty's last ruler had forfeited the

Mandate of Heaven by his tyrannical and licentious behaviour.

At first the Chou sovereigns headed a confederation of city-states linked by kinship ties, which gradually increased their control over the countryside in the Yellow River valley and the North China Plain. Some of these city-states gradually developed into large virtually independent countries, which by the eighth century were giving only nominal allegiance to a much weakened Chou, while *de facto* hegemony was wielded by the most powerful among them. These were times of constant warfare, on three different fronts: first, the alliance of these northern Chinese states had to contend with the large expansionist state of Ch'u in the Yangtze valley, which had its own distinct culture and was not merged with North China until the end of the Chou Dynasty in the third century BC; secondly, these states were subject to harassment by the nomadic peoples living not only beyond the frontiers of Chinese settlement but also within the more mountainous and inaccessible regions of their own territories (just as aboriginal non-Chinese people have continued to occupy areas of China right up to the present day); and thirdly, these states were engaged in internecine conflict in which the smaller were absorbed by the larger until the unification of China by the state of Ch'in in 221 BC and the dawn of the imperial age.

These political changes were closely linked with great social and economic transformations, from hereditary aristocratic rule towards meritocracy, from serfdom towards a free peasantry, from a barter economy towards a widespread use of currency, from aristocratic chariot-warfare towards conflict between huge armies of peasants. But it was not until after Confucius's time that the pace of these changes accelerated so that they sparked off an era of wide-ranging speculation without parallel in Chinese history, as the so-called Hundred Schools sought solutions to the problems of man in society. This was the age of Confucius's great successors, Mencius (*c.* 371–289 BC) and Hsün Tzu (*c.* 298–238 BC); but Confucius himself had lived at a time when it was still possible to look back to a Golden Age rather than forward to a Utopia.

Major Chinese dynasties

Chou ?1027–256 BC

Ch'in 221–206 BC   Ch'in Shih Huang Ti unifies China and builds the Great Wall to defend it from the northern nomads. The Confucian books and much other ancient literature are destroyed in the 'Burning of the Books' in 213 BC, part of Ch'in Shih Huang Ti's totalitarian attempt to wipe out opposition.

Former Han 206 BC – AD 9   This is the first great imperial dynasty. Much of the old literature is recovered and restored, and Confucianism becomes the dominant philosophy and heart of the educational system

Later Han 25–220   Buddhism, the chief foreign rival of Confucianism, is introduced to China.

Sui 581–618   China is reunified after nearly four centuries of division, for most of which time North China has been split between various non-Chinese states

T'ang 618–907   Buddhism is at the height of its influence but Confucian influence is restored as the revived civil service examination system grows in importance.

Sung 960–1279   This is the heyday of Neo-Confucian philosophy, and a period of great technological and industrial progress.

Yüan 1279–1368   China is ruled by Mongols, and Confucianism suffers a setback with the suspension of the examinations for several decades.

Ming 1368–1644   Following Mongol rule, this is a conservative and autocratic regime.

Ch'ing 1644–1912   China is governed by Manchus, whose rulers adopt Confucian culture to show themselves worthy of the Mandate of Heaven. Examinations dominated by Confucian Classics are abolished in 1905.

Note on romanization

I have retained the more familiar Wade-Giles system, which has been used for most English-language books on China, in preference to the new *pinyin* system introduced by the Chinese, which gives even less idea how the words are actually pronounced.

Note on references

References to the *Analects* are given by book and chapter as numbered in Waley's translation; to *Mencius* by the standard enumeration of book and chapter; to Hsün Tzu by the page number in B. Watson's *Hsün Tzu: Basic Writings*; and to the *Record of Rites* by volume and page number of James Legge's translation, which is to be found in volumes 27 and 28 of *Sacred Books of the East*, ed. Max Müller. The references are preceded by the letters A, M, H, and L respectively.

Acknowledgements

I should like to express my gratitude for the helpful suggestions I have received from my wife, from Keith Thomas, the general editor of the series, and from Henry Hardy and Robert Knowles of the Oxford University Press.

Contents

1 Confucius and K'ung Fu-tzu

K'ung Fu-tzu lived 2,500 years ago, but he was not born for the Western world until the late sixteenth century, when his name was Latinised into Confucius, and the message of the ancient Chinese sage was first brought, in somewhat European guise, to the European consciousness. Marco Polo and other medieval European visitors to China had marvelled at the great cities, the teeming market-places, and the huge quantity of shipping which thronged the waterways; but they had been conscious only of the outer manifestations of this rich civilisation, and no Europeans had sampled the wealth of its literature and philosophy before the arrival of the Jesuits.

The Jesuit missionaries reached China in 1583 and established themselves at Peking under the leadership of Matteo Ricci at the beginning of the seventeenth century. It was the general policy of Jesuit missions to try to secure the conversion of a country by first winning the sympathy of its ruler, and Matteo Ricci and his colleagues soon became aware that, to gain the respect of the emperor, they had to make themselves congenial to the scholar-bureaucrats by whom he was surrounded. To achieve this they needed to become Chinese scholars themselves. So, while steeping themselves in the classical literature, they became strongly influenced by the attitudes of the Chinese *literati*, who thought of China as a country governed by philosophers, whose wisdom and virtue derived from the study of the ancient Confucian literature which they had had to master for the purpose of passing the civil service examinations.

The Jesuit version of Confucian doctrine and of the benevolent despotism which, in their view, administered the country in conformity with Confucian doctrine so aroused the admiration of contemporary European thinkers that Confucius himself has been described as 'the patron saint of the Enlightenment'. On the other hand the Protestant missionaries, who came to China in the nineteenth century, could see little to praise in Confucius since he lacked the light of God. Even James Legge, whose monumental work entitled *The Chinese Classics* was so authoritative as to have been reprinted on its hundredth birthday in the middle of the twentieth century, concluded that Confucius 'threw no new light on any of the questions that have a world-wide interest. He gave no impulse to religion. He had no sympathy with progress. His influence has been wonderful, but it will henceforth wane.' So we in the Western world are heirs to two conflicting attitudes to the Chinese sage.

The first work of translation from the Confucian literature was a book entitled *Confucius Sinarum Philosophus, sive Scientia Sinensis*, which was published in Paris by four Jesuit missionaries in the year 1687. It contained a version of the *Analects* of Confucius and of two short works known as the *Great Learning* and the *Mean*, which were extracted from an ancient collection of materials on ritual entitled the *Record of Rites*. Special attention was paid to these texts, together with the book named after Mencius, Confucius's most distinguished successor, since these four books were required reading for the civil service examinations throughout the last six centuries of imperial Chinese history. They had to be studied with the commentary of Chu Hsi, the twelfth-century Neo-Confucian philosopher, rather than with those written nearer Confucius's own time, so European versions too were much influenced by the interpretation of the Neo-Confucian master.

It was not until 1905, in the dying years of the imperial regime, that the old-fashioned civil service examinations were abolished, and the Four Books and other canonical writings yielded to the advance of modern Western knowledge. Even in the late nineteenth century reformers had had to defend their proposals for change by enlisting the support of Confucius. With the advent of the Republic the former veneration of the classical texts was replaced by a new mood of extreme scepticism about knowledge of antiquity. Later still the predominant mood shifted back towards defence of Chinese culture against the inroads of the West, especially after the First World War had exposed the darker side of European culture. This made the Chinese mindful again of the values of their Confucian heritage, and they were glad to throw its ethical superiority into the scales against the material superiority of the West. In Europe too, although nineteenth-century arrogance towards the 'heathen Chinee' had reduced Confucius to a figure of fun in the eyes of the man in the street, he was taken more seriously in the old universities. When they at last began to pay serious attention to Chinese studies, it was the Confucian literature, rather than contemporary affairs, which became the cornerstone of their interests.

The Four Books formed part of a much larger collection of ancient literature called the Thirteen Classics. This corpus, which includes works of poetry, philosophy, and history, as well as ritual texts and a book of divination, was traditionally treated by the Chinese as an entirely separate category of literature, hallowed above the rest as the repository of truth. In antiquity only five of these works had had canonical status: they were the *Book of Changes*, the *Book of History*, the *Book of Songs*, the *Ritual* (which included the *Record of Rites*), and the *Spring and Autumn*. One reason for Confucius's pre-eminence is that he was thought to have had a hand in all of these five works, either as compiler, commentator, or editor.

However, this group of Classics should not be thought of as the special province of a Confucian school. In European writings Confucianism is often referred to as one of the 'three religions' of China, the other two being Taoism and Buddhism; but this gives a very misleading impression of the nature of Chinese religion. 'Three teachings' or 'three doctrines' would be more appropriate translations of the term. A Chinese did not normally adhere to just one of these doctrines. For the vast majority religion consisted of a motley collection of beliefs and practices to which these three schools of thought each made their contributions. The use of the term Confucianism is also misleading, since the Chinese equivalent, *ju chiao*, means 'the doctrine of the literati', so that the name of Confucius does not in fact occur in the title of this school of thought. Far from being the concern of one school, this canonical literature was a curriculum for all: it originated as a collection of material intended to provide an education suitable for the bureaucrats needed to govern the rapidly expanding Chinese empire during the Former Han Dynasty in the second and first centuries BC. The Classics are at the forefront of the literary heritage of the Chinese people as a whole.

Confronted with these ancient classical texts, how are we to isolate and discuss the authentic teachings of Confucius? There are enormous difficulties. Confucius flourished about 500 BC, three centuries before texts can be reliably dated. Long after his time the conception of individual authorship was still not firmly established, so that the names under which ancient philosophical writings are known are generally those of the thinkers to whom the teachings are attributed. These works consequently include not only genuine material assembled by disciples, but also extraneous matter interpolated by those who wished to give their views respectability by foisting them onto a venerable figure from the past. In the book named after Mencius, the great philosopher who was born a century after Confucius's death and who established him as founder of the tradition which was to dominate Chinese thought, Confucius is already venerated as the greatest of the sages in the words 'Ever since man came into this world there has never been anyone greater than Confucius' (M 2a.2). In such circumstances it is not surprising that his name is used prominently in ancient literature as an advertisement for doctrines not necessarily his own. In the *Record of Rites* he is naturally depicted as a great expert on correct ritual, and in the *Book of Filial Piety* he praises filial piety as the chief virtue. In the great Taoist classic *Chuang Tzu*, on the other hand, Confucius is depicted either as a student of Taoism sitting at Lao Tzu's feet, or as an expert on Taoism himself, or alternatively as a trickster and charlatan who curries favour with rulers by means of his nonsensical talk about moral duty and ritual observance. The earliest biography of Confucius was composed by the great historian Ssu-ma Ch'ien, but since he was writing in about 100 BC, almost four centuries after

Confucius's death, it is not surprising that his account is a hotchpotch of material of varying degrees of credibility.

If we want to get as near as possible to the real Confucius, the best thing we can do is look at the *Analects*. This is a collection of sayings and brief anecdotes, which at least has the advantage of treating Confucius as an ordinary human being and shows little trace of the adoration later lavished upon him. Even the *Analects* does not take us very close to the sage, since it is clear from internal evidence that the work was compiled long after his death, apparently by the disciples of disciples, and presumably at a time when a written record was felt necessary to replace fading memories. Surprisingly little familiarity with the book is shown in literature dating from before the Han Dynasty, which began in 206 BC. Mencius clearly had available to him a quite different compilation of sayings: some of the material corresponds closely with passages from the *Analects*, but many more of his references to Confucius are not traceable in the *Analects* at all. Other pre-Han texts also share sayings with the *Analects*, but only once is the *Analects* acknowledged as the source.

The archaic nature of the language and the very rudimentary arrangement of material give an air of authenticity to the work and suggest that the composition is early enough to preserve some of the spirit of Confucius. To the modern reader it appears to be slapdash. Some pieces are duplicated. Some sayings are set in brief anecdotes, but others are so terse and devoid of context that their meaning is very elusive. Some of the sayings are attributed to Confucius's disciples rather than to the Master himself, and it is clear also that much material from alien sources has infiltrated the work. The tenth book, for example, seems to have been extracted from a work on ritual, the conduct advocated in it being attributed to Confucius rather than commended to the attention of the reader, so that the Master is here represented as a stickler for the finicky detail of ceremonious behaviour. Some passages seem to be late and alien to the work since the style in which they are written is uncharacteristically elaborate and sophisticated. It looks as if Books 3–9 (out of a total of twenty books) may form the oldest stratum, but even they may contain later insertions; and although they have a clearer ring of authenticity, it is impossible to vouch for the genuineness of any of the sayings included in them. Nevertheless, in spite of the disparate nature of the material, even some recently published books persist in treating it all as of equal value and trying to extract every ounce of information they can to produce a coherent picture of Confucius and his philosophy.

Caution is necessary, too, in evaluating the biographical material which appears in various sources. Confucius is said to have lived from 551 to 479, but the fact that firm dates are given is cause for suspicion since he lived in an era when the dates of private individuals were not preserved. For example, the dates of Mencius, who lived in the fourth century BC, can only be worked out approximately from evidence drawn from the book named after him. As for Confucius, his death date derives from a legendary account of the capture of a unicorn in 481 BC, which was thought to herald the death of the sage. His birth date was probably worked out from that, since the *Analects* refers to him at the age of seventy and there was a tradition that he actually lived until his seventy-third year. The great French sinologist Henri Maspero felt that he could have lived a quarter of a century later than the traditional dates, but on the other hand he would need to have been born earlier than 551 BC to fit in with some of the references to him in the *Tso Tradition*, which is the only detailed historical account of the period dating from pre-Han times.

Confucius's ancestors are said to have claimed descent from the royal family of the state of Sung, where a member of the royal house of the recently defeated Shang Dynasty had been set up by the Chou conquerors in the eleventh century BC to continue the Shang sacrifices; but this may be just an example of a lofty pedigree being invented to match up to his later eminence. His father died when he was very young and he was brought up in poverty by his mother. As a young man he held office as keeper of granaries and director of public pastures, but is extremely unlikely to have attained to the posts of Minister of Works and Minister of Crime with which the later tradition of his school invested him. He was ambitious to serve in high office in the hope that he could restore to public life the old morality of the founders of the Chou Dynasty; but making no progress in his own state of Lu, which at the time was controlled by usurpers, he travelled from state to state accompanied by some of his disciples, trying to find a more congenial home for his teachings. It became a common practice for philosophers and political advisers to peddle their wares from court to court in this way during the Warring States period, the two centuries of strife which preceded the unification of China by the state of Ch'in in 221 BC, when its ruler inaugurated the first of the great imperial dynasties to govern much of China as we know it today. Failing to make progress in the political arena, Confucius spent the last period of his life as a private teacher, giving instruction to the humbly born as well as to young men of rank, hoping that those who obtained careers in government would be more successful than himself in putting his ideas into effect. He had a son, who predeceased him, and a daughter; otherwise few details of his private life are mentioned in the *Analects*. But despite the fact that the evidence about his life is difficult to evaluate, the *Analects* does give us a glimpse of a credible personality, a man who was brought up in humble circumstances and was prepared to accept poverty rather than compromise his beliefs, a man who never tired of learning and who stuck doggedly to his task ('He's the one who knows it's no good but goes on trying', A 14.41), a man with a strong sense that he had a divinely appointed mission to restore the Way of the revered founders of the Chou Dynasty.

We can never hope to find out what Confucius was really like and precisely what his teachings consisted of. Even the obituaries in this morning's paper do not tell the whole truth about men known to thousands still living. The task of trying to separate the man from the myth is doomed to failure. But the fact that the real Confucius is irretrievable should not be counted a disaster since it was the myth rather than the reality which was important. The story of his life and work provided a model and inspiration for future generations of scholars and teachers.

For greater philosophical interest one has to look at his two famous successors, Mencius and Hsün Tzu. The appeal of the *Analects* is that it gives us a hazy glimpse of the disciples' memory of one whose example was to be set before the intellectuals of the most populous nation on earth. The sayings attributed to him have served as texts to which much of Chinese life and thought have been appended as commentary, and the *Analects* is the oldest record of one who set the pattern for the Confucian society which China has been for much of the time since he lived.

The sayings attributed to Confucius can be manipulated into some sort of coherent philosophy, but the best way to understand the importance of the Master is to ignore the inevitable inconsistencies in the statements attributed to him and to forget about problems of authenticity. Throughout Chinese history before the present century few have questioned the authenticity of even the most hagiographical references to him. The best way of dealing with Confucius is therefore to take some of the most famous and influential sayings, and to try to show both what they meant in the context of late Chou Dynasty China and how the ideas they contain became characteristic features of Chinese thought and culture. Although the reader who has little knowledge of Chinese civilisation may sometimes find these sayings trivial and inconsequential, this method should give him an impression of their formative influence on Chinese civilisation, and hence a heightened understanding of the nature of that civilisation. The method will have the further advantage of affinity with the long Chinese tradition of commentary on classical texts, in which brief passages of the original work alternate with lengthy explanations. This too is how the sayings appeared to many generations of scholars in the examination halls – as isolated quotations set for commentary. Thus we shall be looking at the *Analects* in a more characteristically Chinese way than we would if we attempted a very abstract distillation of Confucius's thought. And since Confucius saw himself primarily as scholar and teacher, it will be appropriate to start with a chapter based on his sayings about education.

2 Learning and teaching

The Master's love of learning

'I silently accumulate knowledge; I study and do not get bored; I teach others and do not grow weary – for these things come naturally to me.' (A 7.2)

'In a hamlet of ten houses there will certainly be someone as loyal and true to his word as I am, but not someone so fond of learning.' (A 5.27)

'At fifteen I set my heart on learning.' (A 2.4)

In spite of all the difficulties inherent in trying to assess the authenticity of the *Analects* and of other material about Confucius, it is impossible to deny that – although there is no telling whether we have a fairly accurate portrait of the Master or one made much glossier by the memory of his disciples – a recognisable personality does shine through the haze. One of the most important ingredients in his make-up was his love of learning. As an old man in his seventies he gave a terse description of the six stages of his life, which will be easier to understand when we meet it later in this book rather than here at the beginning. But at least the first stage is clear enough: at the age of fifteen he devoted his life to learning. This formed the basis of his whole life's work, for when he made no progress in public affairs or in gaining public recognition for his doctrines, he devoted himself solely to the role of private teacher, in order to distribute the fruits of his learning to others who might prove more successful in giving effect to it.

Thus he served as a model and inspiration for countless scholars of the imperial age, who often had to undertake half a lifetime of study before they at last succeeded in passing the civil service examinations – their only hope of playing a part in affairs. If they were unsuccessful in these ambitions, for them too teaching was the only obvious alternative outlet for their talents. The great significance of Confucius in Chinese history is that in many different ways he served as an example for his fellow-countrymen to follow; and the thought of the Master, patiently devoted to learning and not disheartened by his lack of worldly success, must have been an inspiration to many a frustrated scholar in later times.

Even those who were successful in the examinations had to continue with their studies in order to keep fresh the qualities of character which the Classics had instilled into them; and emperors, who had undergone a rigorous Confucian training before ascending the throne, continued to keep scholars at court to expound the Classics to them. If self-sacrifice, following Christ's example, is the key to the Christian message, then learning, after the fashion of the Master, is the vital ingredient of the Confucian message. But, in the case of China, the message did really get across. As Hsün Tzu put it, 'Learning continues until death and only then does it cease' (H 19). Learning was the occupation of a lifetime, and high office could be its reward. More than any other society China has given status to learning.

Learning does not imply bookishness

'A gentleman who, when he eats, avoids seeking to satisfy his appetite to the full and, when he is at home, avoids seeking comfort, who is diligent in deed and cautious in word, and who associates with those who possess the Way and is rectified by them, may be said to be fond of learning.' (A 1.14)

For Confucius, and for the Chinese tradition in general, learning did not usually mean the accumulation of facts for their own sake. It meant the gathering of knowledge for the sake of guiding one's conduct. Therefore a person who had shown himself to have learnt certain moral lessons could be described as 'fond of learning', even if he were not at all bookish. The word *hsüeh*, which is normally translated as 'learning' or 'to study' often means the study and imitation of moral exemplars. Confucius himself was later seen as the kind of moral exemplar who was an appropriate object of *hsüeh* ('study and imitation'). For instance, Mencius is reported to have said: 'As to what I should like, it is to follow the example of [*hsüeh*, study and imitate] Confucius'

(M 2a.2). So the main object of learning was the imitation of models, and an important part of a teacher's role was to act as a model himself and to provide an example of what the morally conscious human being should be like. The importance of following good examples is illustrated in the quotation above when it refers to the gentleman 'who associates with those who possess the Way and is rectified by them'.

It is a commonplace of ancient Chinese literature to equate education with moral training. In the *Book of History* and also in the *Mencius* it is reported that the legendary sage-emperor Shun appointed a Minister of Education to give instruction to the people because they were not observing the five relationships (i.e. the duties involved in the relationships between father and son, ruler and subject, husband and wife, elder brother and younger brother, and friend and friend). And in the nineteenth century it was still widely believed that such moral training was the cure for the ills which had beset the country, so it was urged that colleges should be established in troubled provinces to educate the people in Confucian principles.

The stereotype of the gentleman provided in this quotation also gives prominence to the virtue of frugality which was much admired by Confucius. This virtue was exemplified by his favourite disciple Yen Hui, who remained cheerful although he lived in squalid surroundings and only had a little rice and water to sustain him (A 6.9). Later it was a necessary part of the equipment of that virtuous figure, the poor scholar who strove for examination success despite his humble origins. Confucian frugality stood in stark contrast with the luxury and extravagance of imperial courts.

The Master's love of antiquity

'I transmit but do not create. I have been faithful to and loved antiquity. In this I venture to compare myself to our old P'eng.' (A 7.1)

'If by keeping the old warm one can provide understanding of the new, one is fit to be a teacher.' (A 2.11)

In the opinion of Confucius models which were supremely

worth imitating had to be sought in antiquity. The Master himself lived at a time of social and political instability consequent on the disintegration of the feudal type of society which characterised the early Chou period. Although the Chinese world was still nominally under the leadership of the Chou king, it had long since broken up into independent states. By the time of Confucius's successor Mencius, the age when inter-state tensions were building up to the climax of the unification of China by the state of Ch'in in 221 BC, the obvious response to the prevailing instability was the reunification of China under any one of the independent states; and Mencius himself argued that any ruler who put his teachings into practice would easily win over 'all under Heaven'. But, living almost two centuries earlier, Confucius had thought that the solution to China's social and political problems still lay in a revival of early Chou values. The commonly held doctrine of the Mandate of Heaven meant that the Chou founders had won the approval of Heaven by their virtue and had therefore been granted the right to replace the preceding Shang Dynasty, whose last ruler had forfeited the Mandate because of his evil and tyrannical behaviour. So the obvious reaction, in the view of Confucius, was a general return to those virtues which had secured the Mandate in the first place.

Since China was isolated from other major civilisations and unaware of any great cultural tradition apart from its own, it could not seek a solution to its difficulties by borrowing ideas from another society. It did not have experience of alternative systems of government, such as democracy or oligarchy, so that the only obvious means of salvation was a ruler who would govern virtuously in the manner of the Chou founders and restore unity to 'all under Heaven'. Therefore what was of supreme importance in Confucius's eyes was the investigation and transmission of the correct traditions concerning the Golden Age of antiquity. If there was an ideal Way to be rediscovered, transmission of that ideal was what was needed and creativity was unnecessary – and indeed both arrogant and harmful. As a lover of antiquity and transmitter of its message Confucius compared himself to P'eng, an obscure figure from ancient times whose name was proverbial for longevity, a Chinese equivalent of Methuselah. Men of great age, whose memory reaches far back into the past, are obviously the best equipped to hand down traditions.

However, despite his reverence for the past, Confucius did not believe in a blind and unthinking traditionalism, and this may be clearly seen in the second saying at the beginning of this section. By keeping the old warm one can provide understanding of the new. Although he disclaimed creativity, there is a sort of creativity in using the past to serve the present. This theme echoes down the ages, for later periods of decline were blamed on failure to transmit the truth about the Golden Age of the Chou Dynasty, so that salvation was to be sought by looking again at the ancient texts and trying to discover a more accurate interpretation of them. Thus, for example, the Neo-Confucian movement arose in the late T'ang Dynasty in response to the country's decline after the tragedy of the An Lu-shan Rebellion; and in the late nineteenth century opposing interpretations of Confucius were still used in support of policies to meet the new challenge of the West.

So again we find that Confucius occupied his usual role of exemplar: he was the supreme example of that love of antiquity and eagerness to go on investigating it which was characteristic of the later Chinese intellectual tradition. Throughout imperial Chinese history men looked back on the feudal period of the Chou Dynasty as a Golden Age, and at the forefront of scholarship there stood a tradition of scholarly commentaries on the ancient texts, interpreting their message for contemporary readers. At the same time the Master's words 'I transmit, but do not create' could serve as a motto for traditional Chinese historiography, which always placed great stress on the transmission of documents. The written word was sacred, and the facts would speak for themselves if only they were handed down. But it was equally true that history's purpose was to serve as a moral guide to present conduct; for in the common Chinese metaphor history was a mirror in which men could see their own actions, understand their own motives, and judge their own behaviour. So Chinese history-writing had twin ideals: the past should be thoroughly transmitted, and the past should be used to understand the present. The seeds of both of these ideals could be found in these two sayings attributed to Confucius.

The Master's association with early Chou culture

When the Master was intimidated at K'uang, he said: 'When King Wen [the Cultured King] died, did culture cease to exist? If Heaven had intended to put an end to such culture, a later mortal like myself would not have succeeded in associating himself with it. If Heaven does not yet put an end to this culture, what can the people of K'uang do to me?' (A 9.5)

Confucius was said to have found himself in difficulties in K'uang because he was mistaken for an adventurer called Yang Huo who had previously created a disturbance in that small frontier town. This is one of four occasions during his travels when his life was said to have been endangered, providing appropriate opportunities for sage-like behaviour and utterances. In this passage Confucius is represented as believing that no harm can befall him since he has a Heaven-sent destiny to preserve the cultural values of the Chou founders.

The antiquity which Confucius particularly loved and wished to transmit to his own generation was the period of the founding of the Chou Dynasty about five hundred years before his birth. This was the period of moral excellence which the Master would have liked to see imitated in order to secure a return to a sound political order in China. King Wen was not the actual founder of the Chou Dynasty, but the one who paved the way for its establishment. His name means 'the Cultured King' and it was probably given to him posthumously because of his style of leadership. He is mentioned only twice in the *Analects*, but it is clear that before Confucius's time he was already thought of as an ideal ruler who laid the foundations for the conquest of the preceding Shang Dynasty by his civilisatory achievements. Mencius was a great admirer of King Wen and in the *Mencius* book he is portrayed as a leader whose kindness to the people gained him such widespread support that, although he initially ruled over only a tiny domain, he was able to prepare the ground for the successful conquest of the Shang Dynasty by his son and successor King Wu, 'the Martial King'.

As a result of these early Confucian writings the belief that every successful armed conquest needed to be preceded by a period of cultural preparation became an important feature of Chinese political thought. The idea was that, through their skill in civil administration and the arts of peace, the conquerors built up a store of moral power which helped them to attract and win over the neighbouring peoples, who then welcomed them with open arms. The conception of the ideal ruler as a successful administrator, skilful in the arts of peace, and attractive to the outside world because of the cultural achievements of his regime, a conception already in existence before Confucius's time and adopted by him, has been profoundly influential throughout the course of Chinese history. The civilian ideal continued to prevail, and military virtues were given a very low place in the scale of values. Ideally the enemy should be won over by a display of China's cultural superiority rather than, or prior to, being conquered militarily. Interesting examples of cultural preparation for military conquest can be seen in the course of Chinese history, and indeed the idea was borrowed by the Manchus who, by immersing themselves in the Confucian literature and traditions, were able to commend themselves to the Chinese as a suitable replacement for the decadent Ming Dynasty.

The word *wen*, here translated 'culture', originally meant 'striped', and consequently 'patterned', 'decorated', or 'adorned'. It therefore came to be applied to things which were not mere necessities of existence, but which gave beauty and variety to civilised life and distinguished it from barbarism. It was the attraction of this decorative element in life – the appeal of fine *objets d'art*, or of grand ritual celebrations and musical performances, together of course with the Chinese script (itself a work of art) and the literature written in it – which was thought to dazzle the untutored barbarian and win him over to the Chinese side. So, as far as the Chinese were concerned, the difference between civilisation and barbarism was neither a matter of social or political organisation, nor a question of race or religion. It was entirely a matter of cultural attainment.

Apart from King Wen, Confucius was thought to have had a special regard for the Duke of Chou, the brother of King Wu who acted as regent during the minority of the latter's son and successor King Ch'eng. It was natural that he should have been venerated in the state of Lu, where Confucius lived, since he was traditionally regarded as the founder and first ruler of that state. Accounts of Confucius's own veneration for the Duke of Chou rest on only two passages in the *Analects*, including the lament 'Alas, extreme is my decline; it is long since I dreamt I saw the Duke of Chou!' (A 7.5). There are in fact very few references to him in early texts; and it is not till the *Mencius* that he is treated as such a sage that, like Confucius, it is necessary to explain why he never ruled over 'all under Heaven'. Here in this passage it is King Wen who is shown to be the inspiration of Confucius and the model which a latter-day ruler should aspire to emulate.

The materials for study are within everyone

Kung-sun Ch'ao of Wei asked Tzu-kung: 'From whom did Confucius derive his learning?' Tzu-kung said: 'The Way of Kings Wen and Wu has not yet collapsed to the ground. It is here present among us, and men of wisdom and talent remember the more important principles of the Way, and men who lack wisdom and talent remember its less important principles. So everyone has the Way of Wen and Wu within himself. From whom then does the Master not learn, and yet what regular teacher does he have?' (A 19.22)

'When I walk with two others, I always receive instruction from them. I select their good qualities and follow them, and avoid their bad qualities.' (A 7.21)

'In the presence of a worthy man, think of equalling him. In the presence of a worthless man, turn your gaze within.' (A 4.17)

In the only other reference to King Wen which occurs in the *Analects* a disciple of Confucius called Tzu-kung expresses the conviction that the Way of Wen and Wu has not entirely faded; but the burden of all of these three passages is that, since the object of learning is to learn how to behave, the materials for study are all around us all the time. The constant learning to which Confucius was devoted was aimed at self-improvement as the prerequisite to achieving improvement in others. Since the principal object of education was the moral training of the young, which is obviously also part of the normal parental role, education was naturally regarded not as something novel but as something which had been in existence since the beginning of time. Learning is as much part of our lives as breathing. Indeed learning can occur unconsciously through the unthinking imitation of our neighbours. So it is extremely important to live in the right district. As Confucius put it, 'It is humaneness which is the attraction of a neighbourhood. If from choice a man does not dwell in the midst of humaneness, how can he attain to wisdom?' (A 4.1). Mencius's mother had a legendary reputation for wisdom in choosing the right environment in which to bring up her son. She moved from the vicinity of a market, where Mencius had played all day at being a hawker, to the neighbourhood of a school, under the influence of which the boy abandoned his former pastimes and played at ritual instead (as Confucius was said to have done as a child). But although the moral lessons one learns from parents and from observing neighbours were thought extremely valuable, there are casual references to schools in the *Mencius* and other early sources, and it was taken for granted in antiquity that formal education had existed for as long as society had existed. Mencius himself quotes the *Book of History* saying: 'Heaven sent down the people who are on earth below, provided rulers for them, and provided teachers for them' (M 1b.3).

Education should be available to all

'From the bringer of a bundle of dried meat upwards, I have never refused instruction to anyone.' (A 7.7)

When the Master went to Wei, Jan Yu drove his carriage. 'How dense is the population!' exclaimed the Master. 'When the people have multiplied, what more should be done for them?' asked Jan Yu. 'Enrich them', he replied. 'And when they have been enriched?' 'Educate them', replied the Master. (A 13.9)

'If there is education there are no class-distinctions.' (A 15.38)

A bundle of dried meat was an extremely humble offering, but Confucius, who endured poverty in his own youth, was prepared to teach anyone who showed a genuine willingness and capacity to learn. The principle that education should be readily available to all who seek it follows naturally from the idea that all men are born equal in the sense that every man has the innate capacity to develop into a sage. This belief was expressly held by Mencius, who declared that 'Everyone may become a Yao or Shun' (M 6b.2). Although Confucius did not express himself so clearly on the subject, there are indications that he inclined in this direction and believed that men were naturally close to each other and were set far apart from each other by their different experiences of life (see quotation on p. 42). So environmental factors like a person's economic situation and education are extremely important; and in equity all should receive both an adequate livelihood so that, freed from want, they can cultivate the virtues, and an equal opportunity of education so that they can fully develop their potential. Mencius was also a powerful advocate of these policies, but they could be traced back to Confucius, as can be seen in his replies to Jan Yu.

Confucius is credited with being the earliest man in China to have accepted these principles. He was more interested in the pupils' eagerness to learn than in their class status, and the majority of the disciples referred to in the *Analects* seem to have come from relatively humble backgrounds. As a consequence of this example set by Confucius the ideal of a nation-wide educational system was set before the Chinese long before other peoples had such a conception. In pre-modern conditions this could never lead to a serious attempt at the introduction of universal education, but it gave a stimulus to the widespread establishment of schools in response to imperial exhortations. As a result of their studies with Confucius his pupils, however humble, were equipped to hold important official appointments. Similarly in late imperial China, when the civil service examination system was well established, the humble could obtain advancement in the government, since entry to the civil service through competitive examination was open to all males, with the exception of members of certain disadvantaged professions, which included actors and policemen.

The third quotation, consisting of a mere four characters in the original, is so condensed that its meaning is not entirely clear. The word *lei*, translated as 'class-distinctions', has a wider sense and means simply 'categories' or 'classification'. Indeed one commentator thought that it meant that there should be no distinction of race, so that it could be taken as an injunction to propagate Confucianism among the barbarians. But the saying has generally been adopted as a slogan for classless education, and as such it used to be displayed on school buildings in China.

The extent to which the humble could achieve greatness through study was always of course limited by economic factors, but there were cases of men from very humble backgrounds rising to the very top of the civil service, and there are many edifying accounts of ambitious scholars studying at night while supporting their widowed mothers by day. Many talented but poor young men received an education through the charity of wealthy relatives or in village schools financed by the more prosperous local farmers. Many combined a life of scholarship with agricultural labour, or 'ploughed with the writing-brush', as it was sometimes called. And as inspiration for all this the Chinese would look back to the one who thought there should be no class-distinction in education and was prepared to teach anyone, however poor, who would respond to his message.

Subjects taught by the Master

The Master took four subjects for his teaching: culture, conduct, loyalty, and good faith. (A 7.24)

'Young men should be filial when at home and respectful to elders when away from home. They should be earnest and keep their promises. They should extend their love to all, but be intimate only with the humane. If they have any energy to spare after the performance of these duties, they should use it to study 'culture'. (A 1.6)

There are, in the *Analects*, various references to the topics included in Confucius's teaching, all of which he saw as contributing to the moral training of the individual. The standard content of education in antiquity was known as the six arts. These were rites, music, archery, charioteering, writing and mathematics, a collection of subjects of largely practical value essential to the upbringing of the young aristocrat. It was not at all a literary type of education, and only under the heading of 'rites' would there be any place for the kind of moral training in which Confucius specialised. For Confucius, too, literature was of no importance except in so far as it served the purpose of moral training. It was as a consequence of the teachings of Hsün Tzu that the Confucian approach to education developed the bookishness which was characteristic of the imperial age: he wrote that 'education begins with the recitation of the Classics and ends with the reading of ritual texts' (H 19), and it was he who recommended a list of Classics which were to become the nucleus of the curriculum for budding bureaucrats under the Former Han Dynasty, thus establishing the pattern for an educational system which would always set great store by the canonical writings.

Of the subjects listed, loyalty and good faith will have to be considered later in connection with the other Confucian virtues. The importance of culture for Confucius's teaching has already been noted. It was the culture of the Chou founders, the hallmark of civilisation which distinguished the Chinese from the untutored barbarians by whom they were surrounded, that Confucius was anxious to preserve and restore. Although this is an essential component of Confucius's message, he sometimes seemed to subordinate it to a man's duty to fulfil his social obligations. The study of culture was only to be pursued if there was energy to spare from such more serious occupations, as the second quotation indicates. But although Confucius seemed to make a distinction between moral self-cultivation and the pursuit of the polite arts and put the latter in a secondary position, it is clear from other passages that culture was a very important element of the moral training necessary for the production of ideal gentlemen to administer a harmonious society (A 6.25). Yen Hui, the favourite disciple, also claimed that the Master had broadened him with culture (A 9.10).

The Master's use of the Songs

'One is roused by the *Songs*, established by ritual, and perfected by music.' (A 8.8)

'My young friends, why do none of you study the *Songs*? The *Songs* may be used to stimulate emotions, to observe people and share their company, and to express grievances. At home they enable one to serve one's father, and abroad to serve one's ruler.' (A 17.9)

'A man may know by heart the three hundred *Songs*, but if he is given a post in government and cannot successfully carry out his duties, and if he is sent to far places and cannot report in detail on his mission, then even if he has learnt to recite many of them, of what use is this to him?' (A 13.5)

Other important materials for study are the *Songs*, ritual and music. The *Book of Songs* is a collection of poems which had already become part of the common literary heritage before Confucius's time. The traditional account of its completion is that Confucius selected 305 out of 3,000 poems which had been assembled by a music master of the state of Lu, but it is extremely unlikely that he had anything to do with the selection or editing of the pieces. The work was advocated by Hsün Tzu in his educational programme and in the Former Han Dynasty it was given the status of a Classic; and the alleged link with Confucius obviously derives from the fact that, once he began to be revered as a sage, his role in the establishment of the classical tradition was bound to be greatly exaggerated.

The *Book of Songs* consists partly of folk songs and partly of formal odes used for ceremonial occasions. It has considerable literary appeal, in this respect surpassing everything else which has come down to us from the Chou Dynasty, but it is not this aspect of the *Songs* which interested Confucius. Indeed the Master showed no interest in literature as such or any awareness that writing could be appreciated for its aesthetic appeal. All study, even of literature, is undertaken for a purely practical purpose. My translation of the difficult second sentence of the second quotation in the above group is somewhat tentative, but the whole passage certainly shows that the *Songs* were considered by Confucius to heighten a man's sensibilities and enable him the better to perform the social duties which were his primary responsibility. Also, in dealing with the *Songs*, Confucius did not forget that the ultimate aim of education was to obtain a post in government. As the final quotation insists, it is no use being able to recite the three hundred *Songs* unless this fits one for the task of administration and diplomacy.

The specific reason why a knowledge of the *Songs* was helpful to statesmanship is that quotations were used to oil the wheels of diplomatic exchanges. It was conventionally accepted that the words could be taken out of context and made to bear any meaning required by the speaker. Some idea of the technique can be gained by seeing how Confucius used the book for educational purposes. For example, there is a passage in the *Songs* which runs: 'As cut, as filed, as chiselled, as polished'. It is a simile referring to the jade-like elegance of a princely young lover, but for educational purposes it must be given a more high-minded interpretation, so when it is quoted in the *Analects* the simile is used to refer to the polishing and refinement of a man's character (A 1.15). As a result of this use of the expression in the *Analects*, it became a stock reference in Chinese literature for moral refinement rather than the physical elegance intended in the original poem. The disciple Tzu-kung received the Master's congratulations on this reinterpretation of the passage, which amounts to a deliberate misconstruction of the lines for the purpose of using them as a moral tag. The use of this kind of device enabled courtiers and diplomats to refer guardedly and obliquely to delicate and dangerous topics and so feel their way towards solutions which blunt and straightforward language might have rendered impossible.

In such exchanges the meanings of words could, if necessary, be completely altered. For example, the Master said: 'If out of the three hundred *Songs* I took one phrase to cover their meaning, it would be "Let there be no depravity in your thoughts"' (A 2.2). But in fact this comes from a description of horses and the words taken here to mean 'no depravity' meant 'without swerving' in the original context, while the word rendered as 'thoughts' does not carry that sense in the passage in the *Songs*, but is merely used as an exclamation. This particular example of Confucius's technique is interesting not only because he uses this device of misinterpretation, but also because the end product, 'Let there be no depravity in your thoughts', firmly indicates that Confucius thought of the *Songs* as a sourcebook for moral training. Many of the *Songs* are simple love poems, but these had to be given a more solemn interpretation befitting the dignity of their inclusion in the canon of Five Classics during the Former Han period, especially as Confucius was thought responsible for selecting them from a much larger corpus of poems. The Master himself had provided a technique of reinterpretation, so such poems were generally misconstrued as allusions to the loyalty inherent in the ruler-minister relationship which was at the heart of Confucian ethics, rather than as descriptions of the dalliance of lovers.

Another classic which has been especially closely associated with Confucius is the *Spring and Autumn* annals, which, like the *Book of Songs*, was incorporated in the canon in the Former Han Dynasty. There is no reference to the work in the *Analects* itself, but in the *Mencius* Confucius is reported to have made the prophetic statement 'It is the *Spring and Autumn* which will make men understand me; it is the *Spring and Autumn* which will make men condemn me.' Later Mencius went on to say: 'When Confucius completed the *Spring and Autumn*, rebellious ministers and unruly sons were struck with terror.' The *Spring and Autumn* is a sparse, annalistic account of the state of Lu, which Confucius was traditionally believed to have compiled, indicating by subtle variations in the use of language his praise or blame for the participants in the historical events described.

In fact no such theory about the composition of the *Spring and Autumn*, or at any rate of the work which at present goes under that name will survive careful scrutiny; so it is probable that the Master merely used the book as a source from which to illustrate his message and demonstrate the decadence of the age.

Later, as I have already mentioned, it became one of the principal aims of traditional Chinese historians to hold up a mirror to mankind, so that the acts of famous and notorious historical characters might provide examples for later men either to follow or to avoid. This tradition mainly derived from the conventional interpretation of the *Spring and Autumn*, and was especially evident in biographical writing. The standard dynastic histories each have biographical sections, which give accounts of the public careers of the prominent men of the age; and the value of these accounts is not so much that they portray the truth about the individuals concerned, but that they give examples of what their successors in public life should imitate or avoid. Since learning primarily consisted of the accumulation of knowledge for the purpose of guiding one's conduct, the reading of history shared this aim; and the classical example of this attitude to history, which had a powerful influence on later historical writing, was the *Spring and Autumn*, which was traditionally attributed to Confucius. So in connection with both the *Spring and Autumn* and the *Songs* Confucius served as the earliest exemplar of the use of literature for moral purposes.

It is clear from his references to the *Book of Songs* that Confucius had no conception of literature as a subject of independent enquiry and interest. The *Songs* were merely a tool of diplomacy and a guide to morality and social conduct. It would have been surprising if it had been otherwise, for after the *Book of Songs* there was an extraordinary lack of poetry and of other writing for purely literary purposes right through until the end of the Chou Dynasty. Throughout imperial Chinese history literature's *raison d'être* was generally conceived as the teaching of truth and virtue, so Confucian bureaucrats tried to restrict the influence of popular plays and novels which disregarded the orthodox morality. Such attitudes lingered on, and it was still as true under the regime of Chairman Mao as it had been in ancient China that politics was in command and that literature was its servant.

3 Ritual and music

The importance of ritual in government

'If one can govern a country by ritual and deference, there is no more to be said; but if one cannot govern a country by ritual and deference, then what has one to do with ritual?' (A 4.13)

In the previous chapter there is a quotation from the *Analects* in which Confucius is reported to have said that one is 'aroused by the *Songs*, established by ritual, and perfected by music'; and it is now time to consider the part played by ritual in Confucius's teaching, and its impact on later Chinese thought. The individual was 'established by ritual' and so it was an important tool in the process of self-cultivation; but ultimately, like a knowledge of the *Book of Songs*, it was only valuable in so far as it assisted in the government of the country.

The word *li*, translated here as 'ritual', originally meant 'to sacrifice', and so its first extension of usage was restricted to ritual in the context of religion. Later, however, the meaning spread to include ceremonious behaviour in secular contexts, initially at those important occasions which were imbued with quasi-religious solemnity, such as court audiences, the reception of envoys from other states, challenges to battle, archery contests, and the like. At such events a ritualised protocol and code of behaviour had to be observed; and from use on such ceremonial occasions *li* became further diffused so that it coloured all social occasions and all human relationships, in such everyday contexts meaning 'propriety', 'politeness', or 'good form'. The virtue of deference or yielding (*jang*), which is associated with ritual in this passage, could also be used in ordinary social intercourse, to mean 'yielding precedence'; but its main significance in Confucian ethics is that it is the characteristic quality of the ruler who cedes his throne to a successor chosen for his virtue, for which the model was the legendary sage-emperor Yao's abdication in favour of Shun. It is the opposite of self-assertiveness and so a virtue which is valuable in government and diplomacy as well as in social relations.

The importance of ritual in Chinese society may partly be due to the fact that the Chinese did not share our concept of a divine law-giver, so that human conduct had to depend much more on codes of behaviour based on precedent (as well as on the imitation of models, the importance of which has already been stressed in connection with education). At the same time the early Chou sovereigns had been overlords of a vast area of present-day north China at a time of primitive communications, so the political system of this period depended very heavily on the family ties which linked the rulers of the various states which recognised their suzerainty; and this cohesiveness could be more securely preserved if the family links and social hierarchies involved were solemnised and reinforced by a code of conduct which was heavily imbued with ritual. So ritual, which had originally been entirely devoted to the service of the spirits, became a means of controlling social behaviour and preserving political hierarchies.

This preoccupation with ritual is not solely a Chinese concern. We are familiar with a similar concept in our own society, a ceremoniousness ranging from the pomp displayed on grand royal occasions or important military parades to the ordinary courtesies of the informal handshake or the polite gesture of deference; but with us ritual is not carried to such extremes of detail, nor is it codified and treated as an all-embracing system, as it has been by the Chinese. There are other important differences. For example, *li* 'ritual' has something in common with mores, but the word 'mores' is used to mean the customary norms of a particular society, whereas the Chinese, being unfamiliar with other advanced societies, considered *li* to be universally valid. Another way in which ritual was more pervasive in the Chinese system than in ours was that it was not sufficient just to repeat the appropriate words and perform the appropriate actions. There was an added dimension to the performance of *li*: each rite had to be accompanied by the appropriate attitude, and there evolved a rich vocabulary describing the various ritual postures and expressions. These words were sometimes used to describe people's appearance, not only when performing ceremonies, but also when engaged in the ordinary business of life. An example from Book 10 of the *Analects*, the section which seems to have been extracted from a work on ritual, will give an impression of how *li* pervades the most trivial activities:

In bed he does not lie in the posture of a corpse. When at home he does not use ritual attitudes. When he sees anyone in mourning, even if he knows him well, he must change countenance; and when he sees anyone in sacrificial garb, or a blind man, even if he is in informal dress, he must be sure to adopt the appropriate attitude. On meeting anyone in deep mourning he must bow across the bar of his carriage; he also bows in the same way to people carrying official tablets. When he is given a dish of delicacies, he must change countenance and rise to his feet. At a sudden clap of thunder or a violent gust of wind he must change countenance. (A 10.16)

In the ancient Chinese world Confucius must have been seen by the many who could not appreciate his moral and political teachings as primarily a specialist on ritual. In the *Tso Tradition*, the main historical source for the period, he is referred to as a teacher of ritual; and on one occasion, when a ruler consulted him about the advisability of attacking another state, the Master is reported to have said that he had learnt about sacrificial vessels and not about warfare, and then to have left the state in a huff, declaring: 'The bird chooses its tree; the tree does not choose the bird' (Duke Ai, year 11; see also A 15.1 for a briefer version). It became a cliché of biographical writing that a great man's career was foreshadowed by his youthful activities; and, sure enough, Ssu-ma Ch'ien's biography shows the boy Confucius playing at arranging sacrificial vessels and performing ceremonies. In the *Record of Rites* the Master naturally appears as an expert on ritual, and in the *Analects* there is much evidence of his concern with this subject, although apparently not enough to please some of his followers, who seem to have inserted the material in

Book 10 to provide more detail on the Master's ritual postures and attitudes.

The correct performance of ritual by the ruler was held to be essential to the welfare of the state. The ancient belief in the interaction between heaven and earth meant that, not only in the Chou period but also throughout the imperial age, it was thought that the correct performance of the appropriate rituals by the Son of Heaven was necessary to secure the harmonious operation of the cosmos. Ritually incorrect actions by the Son of Heaven were bound to be followed by natural disasters. Confucius saw the regretted decline from the standards of early Chou culture partly in terms of departure from appropriate rituals. During his time the powers of the Duke of Lu, his own state, had largely been taken over by three families; and the head of one of these families was described by Confucius as intolerable for usurping the ruler's prerogative of having eight teams of dancers performing at a ceremony (A 3.1). But although he did show his deep concern that such matters of detail should be correct, he was much more involved with the fundamental principles and meaning of *li* than with the outward forms. He stressed the ethical significance of ritual and saw it as a means of bringing order into the life of the individual and into his relations with the family and his dealings with society as a whole, so that one is 'established by ritual'. If the emotions and attitudes of mind associated with religious ceremonies could be carried over into the secular world, this would strengthen and beautify human relationships.

The words 'employ the people as though you were officiating at a great sacrifice' (A 12.2, see also p. 40) encapsulate the important Confucian view that the sacred is not something set apart from ordinary life, but something which one should be conscious of in all life's activities. Confucius appreciated that ritual was a powerful device for securing the harmonious human order which he craved; so he constantly stressed the important role of ritual in government, suggesting, as in the opening quotation, that ritual was useless unless it was employed in governing the country, for that was the supreme task for which it was most vitally needed. So he maintained that 'if the ruler loves ritual, then the people will be easy to employ' (A 14.44), an idea which is spelt out more fully in the *Mean*, where the Master says: 'If a ruler understands the rites at the altars of Heaven and Earth and comprehends the meaning of the ancestral sacrifices, then ruling his kingdom will be as easy as pointing to the palm of his hand' (Ch. 19).

The relationship between ritual and humaneness

'If a man is not humane, what has he to do with ritual? If a man is not humane, what has he to do with music?' (A 3.3)

Yen Hui asked about humaneness. The Master said: 'To subdue oneself and return to ritual is humane. If for one day a ruler could subdue himself and return to ritual, then all under Heaven would respond to the humaneness in him. For does humaneness proceed from the man himself, or does it proceed from others?' Yen Hui said: 'I beg to ask for the details of this'. The Master said: 'Do not look at what is contrary to ritual, do not listen to what is contrary to ritual, do not speak what is contrary to ritual, and make no movement which is contrary to ritual.' (A 12.1)

The omnipresence of ritual in all kinds of social situations raises the question of its relationship to the social virtues. Here are two passages in which ritual is related to humaneness, the chief of the Confucian virtues, which will be discussed in more detail in the following chapter. From the first of these quotations it is clear that Confucius gives priority to humaneness. Humaneness is the essential virtue, and ritual (which could, after all, be conducted with regard for form rather than meaning) is, as stated elsewhere in the *Analects*, 'secondary' (A 3.8). The social virtues are thus the foundation on which ritual must be built. On the other hand in conversation with Yen Hui the Master says that 'to subdue oneself and return to ritual is humane', so that in this passage ritual is being given primacy and humaneness is being defined in terms of adherence to it. This conflict illustrates the difficulty of interpreting Confucius's thought on the basis of the *Analects*. One could argue that the two passages are not in serious conflict with each other but merely illustrate the close links which are bound to exist between the supreme virtue of humaneness and the Confucian conception of ritual, with its important role in social relationships. On the other hand it is equally true that the second passage comes from Book 12, and so may be a later interpolation emanating from a source which, like Hsün Tzu, elevates ritual to a supreme position. Certainly this passage's insistence that one should heed the dictates of ritual in every word and deed could be taken as a source of inspiration by extreme ritualists and could help to give Confucius the reputation of being an unsophisticated stickler for the empty forms of ritual.

The sterile pursuit of ritual expertise for its own sake was an inevitable consequence of the inability of lesser minds to comprehend the true virtues of Confucius's conception of ritual. When so much of human behaviour was subject to the demands of ritual, it tended to become mere habit; and the empty show of ritual, especially if accompanied by extravagance, was an easy target for criticism, so that in hostile writings Confucius was tarred with the same brush as the less perceptive of his followers.

On the other hand the discussion of the relationship between *li* and the social virtues was carried further by Mencius, who concerned himself with the nature of the human personality which was reflected by these social virtues. He regarded *li* (together with humaneness, dutifulness and wisdom) as one of the four basic virtues which derive from the cultivation of four so-called 'shoots' or 'sprouts' – as essential a part of the human personality as the four limbs are an essential part of the human body. Hsün Tzu had an even grander conception of *li*. Confucius had claimed for *li* a vital role in social relationships and in government as well as in religion, and *li*, unlike mores, was thought to have universal validity, so Hsün Tzu took the matter a stage further and elevated *li* to the status of a cosmic principle. 'Heaven and Earth gave birth to the *li*', he declared, and it was his view that the social distinctions and the rules of conduct whereby men observed them were as natural as the four seasons. 'Through rites', he declared, 'Heaven and Earth join in harmony, the sun and moon shine, the four seasons proceed in order, the stars and constellations march, the rivers flow and all things flourish, men's likes and dislikes are regulated and their joys and hates made appropriate' (H 94).

A statement on the supreme importance of *li* is attributed to Confucius in the *Record of Rites*: 'Of all things to which the people owe their lives the rites are the most important. If it were not for the rites, they would have no means of regulating the services paid to the spirits of Heaven and Earth; if it were not for the rites, they would have no means of distinguishing the positions of ruler and subject, high and low, old and young; if it were not for the rites, they would have no means of differentiating the relationships between male and female, between father and son, and between elder and younger brother, and of linking far and near by the ceremony of marriage' (L 2.261). By the incorporation of this work into the classical canon in the Former Han Dynasty the place of ritual was firmly established in the educational and governmental tradition of imperial China. Just as in antiquity Confucius and others of his kind (rather than priests) were the experts on ritual, both in its religious and in its secular manifestations, so the literati, educated in the Confucian Classics (which included the ritual texts), were the experts on ritual throughout imperial Chinese history. As such they, rather than any priesthood, played their part in the religious ritual authorised by the state. Among the common people in late imperial China the concept of *li* was propagated by the widespread dissemination of such works as Chu Hsi's *Family Rituals*, which were often commended in the rules published by clans for the edification of their members. And in the apparatus of bureaucracy the Board of Rites took its place alongside the Boards of Civil Office, Revenue, Punishments, War, and Works as one of the six government departments which remained a constant feature of the imperial administrative system.

Ceremoniousness and excessive politeness were features of Chinese civilisation which became a familiar part of the European image of China, and the language – with its many honorific and humilific expressions – was exploited for its

quaintness by European writers. But beneath these superficialities there lies something deeply important, a philosophy
which embraced within the one concept of *li* all rituals and
ceremonies, whether religious or secular, as well as all common
acts of politeness. At its finest this concept could give added
dignity and meaning to ordinary human relationships. In this
sphere too Confucius has been regarded as the chief inspiration.
Not only because of the many references to *li* in the *Analects*, but
also because the *Record of Rites* and other ancient sources treat
him as an expert on *li*, Confucius has been regarded as the chief
mentor of the Chinese people in matters of ritual.

Mourning rites and music

Lin Fang asked about the main principles to be observed in connection
with ritual. The Master said: 'An important question indeed! In ritual
it is better to be frugal than lavish. In mourning rites it is better to be
sorrowful than fearful.' (A 3.4)

Tsai Yü asked about the three years' mourning, and said that one year
was already long enough. 'If gentlemen do not practise the rites for three
years,' he said, 'the rites will certainly decay. If for three years they do
not make music, music will certainly die. In a year the old crops have
gone and the new crops have come up, so after a completed year the
mourning should stop'. The Master said: 'If you were then to eat good
rice and wear embroidered clothes, would you feel at ease?' 'Yes', he
replied. 'If you would be at ease, then do so', said the Master. 'But when
a gentleman is in mourning, if he eats dainties he does not relish them,
and if he hears music he does not enjoy it, and if he sits in his usual place
he is not at ease. That is why he abstains from these things. But if you
feel at ease, then do them!' When Tsai Yü had left, the Master said:
'How inhumane Yü is! It is not until a child is three years old that it
leaves its parents' arms. The three years' mourning is the mourning
universally adopted by all under Heaven. Surely Yü had those three
years of parental love?' (A 17.21)

Before we leave this important topic of ritual here are two more
examples of its treatment in the *Analects*. The response to the
disciple Lin Fang shows that Confucius believed that rites
should be informed with genuine emotion and should not be

conducted with extravagant display. Frugality became a strong Confucian tradition, and Mencius was constantly critical of rulers for taking people away from productive labours on the land to provide them with luxuries. But the tradition of frugality has run counter not only to the luxuriousness of imperial courts, but also to the desire of ordinary individuals in Chinese society to impress the neighbours at times of importance in family history such as weddings and funerals.

The conversation with Tsai Yü, a disciple in whom Confucius was much disappointed, is in a style which seems to indicate that it is a late addition to the text. The passage claims Confucius's support for the three years' mourning, a practice which was probably not very ancient and was by no means universal, as Confucius is reported to have stated. The justification attributed to the Master is absurd, as also is Tsai Yü's attack on the practice; but it appears not only in the *Analects* but also in the section of the *Record of Rites* dealing with the three years' mourning (Book 35). Consequently the Master's support for the three years' mourning became enshrined in the Confucian tradition; and this was sufficient to ensure that the practice became mandatory, so that even men in high office had to resign and return home to mourn for their parents. Although the practice is known as the three years' mourning, according to the *Record of Rites* it should only last for twenty-seven months, so a more accurate translation would be 'mourning unto the third year'.

Music is, as often, mentioned in parallel with ritual in the conversation with Tsai Yü. There is a further reference to music in the same conversation: the Master says that, when in mourning, the gentleman does not enjoy music. Confucius himself is said to have been fond of music. He played the zithern and sang (A 7.31 and 17.20). The words for 'enjoy' and 'music' are written with the same character, so that 'enjoy music' and 'enjoy enjoyments' or 'enjoy entertainments' are written identically in ancient Chinese. There is a passage in *Mencius* which puns on the two meanings. A king expresses his anxiety about his love of music, because he feels embarrassed that he can only appreciate the popular music of the day and not the music of antiquity. Mencius's response is typical: it does not matter what kind of music the king enjoys as long as he shares his music/enjoyments with the people (M 1b.1).

The ancient Chinese were indeed fully conscious of the sheer joy obtained from listening to music and the powerful effect it had on the emotions. But there was something far more valuable in music than the mere provision of pleasure. It is often closely associated with ritual, as in Tsai Yü's opening remarks, for ritual ceremony did often include dance, mime and music. Hence it was thought that just as the ancient kings established ritual practices which assisted in the maintenance of cosmic harmony, they also sponsored the composition of music which had a similarly beneficial effect. It was taken for granted that sound could have magical influences. There was a story current in antiquity which illustrated the dramatic effect that music could have. A certain ruler wished to listen to a piece of music which his music master said he was not worthy to hear since he was deficient in virtue. When he insisted in spite of his music master's warning, black clouds came up in the west, and a fierce wind was followed by violent rain that tore the curtains and hangings, overturned the cups and bowls, and shook tiles down from the roof. Afterwards his country suffered a great drought for three years, and sores broke out all over the ruler's body. Some music was also considered wild and licentious, so that it could have devastating effects not only on human personality but also on cosmic order. It was therefore a vital necessity of statecraft to institute the playing of music which fostered the harmony of the cosmos.

The influence of ritual music was especially great at the time of important cosmic events like the solstices. The *History of the Former Han Dynasty* has a description of the playing of cosmic music at the time of the winter solstice. This music was intended to facilitate the passage from *yin* to *yang* which took place at that particular season. There is a parallel here between music and architecture. The ancient ritual texts indicated how the capital city should be laid out to conform with the cardinal directions, so that the heart of the political system was patterned on the cosmic order. Music did for time what architecture did for space; for appropriate music and ritual were performed to accompany the cosmic events which marked the passage of the seasons. Music therefore had the most profound significance. When he heard the Shao music, Confucius is said not to have 'known the taste of meat' for three months, and to have exclaimed that he did not picture that music-making could have attained to such a level (A 7.13). This extraordinary impact on the Master did not mean that he was bowled over by aesthetic pleasure. Obviously the music referred to must have been of great ritual importance. According to later tradition it was the music that accompanied the dance miming the peaceful accession of the legendary sage-emperor Shun, which was an event of great cosmic importance: his matchless qualifications for ruling over all under Heaven would ensure harmony not merely on earth, but in Heaven as well.

Because of the close integration between the human and the cosmic order music was naturally also important in the lives of individual human beings. By ensuring that his people listened to the right kind of music a ruler could cultivate harmony and virtue among them. So rites and music stand side by side as the means whereby the ruler could transform and complete the nature of his people. That is why, in the first quotation on p. 21, Confucius says: 'One is roused by the *Songs*, established by ritual, and perfected by music.' Music has a detached, magical, cosmic quality, which completes the task of bringing human beings in tune with the cosmic harmonies.

4 Humaneness and other virtues

The nature of humaneness

Fan Ch'ih asked about humaneness. The Master said: 'It is to love others.' (A 12.22)

Tzu-chang asked Confucius about humaneness. Confucius said: 'He who could put five things into practice everywhere under Heaven would be humane.' Tzu-chang begged to ask what they were and he replied: 'Courtesy, generosity, good faith, diligence and kindness. If you behave with courtesy, then you will not be insulted; if you are generous, then you will win the multitude; if you are of good faith, then other men will put their trust in you; if you are diligent, then you will have success; and if you are kind, then you will be able to command others.' (A 17.6)

The chapters on education and ritual have included several references to virtues, including humaneness. Indeed the quotations which introduce the topic of ritual revealed a close link between it and humaneness, for the Master said: 'To subdue oneself and return to ritual is humane,' and again 'If a man is not humane, what has he to do with ritual?' The link with education is also close. Since according to the Confucian tradition education was primarily concerned with learning how to behave, it was natural that Confucius and his followers should have developed an interest in man's moral capacities and evolved theories about the general characteristics of human nature. This has in fact been one of the fundamental concerns of Confucian philosophy, and much later discussion is focused on *jen* (humaneness), which first appeared as a term of philosophical importance and interest in the pages of the *Analects*.

The problem of translating Chinese ethical terms is very great. Whatever English words are used are bound to have their own special associations which are alien to Chinese attitudes. For *jen* nobody has found an entirely satisfactory solution. Benevolence, love, altruism, kindness, charity, compassion, magnanimity, perfect virtue, goodness, human-heartedness, humaneness, humanity, and man-to-manness have all been used. One scholar even coined the word 'hominity', which certainly has the merit of avoiding irrelevant associations, but outlandish neologisms can never provide an answer to problems of translation, which are at their most insoluble in an area like moral philosophy, where a deep knowledge of the culture is necessary before one can understand all the implications of the terms used. Waley's version of *jen* is 'Goodness' and Legge translates it as 'perfect virtue'. Both versions do justice to the fact that *jen* is the supreme virtue in the *Analects*, but they sacrifice the etymological connection with *jen* meaning 'man'. So although 'goodness' (and 'benevolence' for *jen* in *Mencius*) often provides a close and smooth translation, for the purpose of more serious study it is preferable to use the words 'humane' and 'humaneness' and try to clear one's mind of the inappropriate associations which cling to them and think only of the essential meaning of the words. Basically *jen* means the manifestation of ideal human nature; and since Confucian ethics is concerned not so much with qualities of mind and heart as with activities and not so much with man in isolation as with man relating to his fellow human beings, so that man's virtues are social virtues manifested in the conduct of human relationships, then *jen* may be defined as dealing with other human beings as a man ideally should. Although Confucius was concerned that a man should achieve individual perfection, the achievement of that perfection was impossible in isolation from society. It needed to be manifested in dealing with others. This is even demonstrated in the construction of the character for *jen*, which is written with two elements, man + two, thus constituting a kind of shorthand for human relationships, which the translation 'man-to-manness' tries to render literally.

Humaneness is obviously closely related to other social virtues like filial piety. Indeed filial piety and brotherly respect are specifically described in the *Analects* as the roots of *jen* (A 1.2), but the words are attributed not to Confucius but to his disciple Yu Tzu, and they appear in the first book, which gives a disproportionate amount of attention to filial piety and probably belongs to a later stratum of the book compiled when that virtue was in the ascendant. The simplest description of *jen* in the *Analects* is that given in the reply to the disciple Fan Ch'ih, 'to love others'; but, as the supreme virtue and sum of human moral achievements, it may be analysed into various components, as in the reply to the disciple Tzu-chang. From this description it is clear that 'altruism' is not a satisfactory translation. Humaneness is not entirely selfless. The social virtues have their give and take. Just as filial piety is rewarded with parental care, so humane rule is rewarded by the allegiance of the people.

An important part of learning was, as we have seen, the imitation of exemplars, so an important part of moral education would be the discussion of what contemporary or historical paragons could be described as showing exemplary adherence to humaneness or one of the other virtues. The word *jen* – used here as an adjective (humane) rather than as a noun (humaneness) – would be an appropriate label to attach to someone proverbially responsible for supremely virtuous behaviour, someone who has dealt with other human beings as a man ideally should. It was not the kind of virtue which, like filial piety, could be unpacked into a list of specific duties. It was the supreme accolade for moral behaviour. So for Confucius's disciples a stock question was whether so-and-so could be described as *jen* (humane).

Unfortunately, however, they seem to have found difficulty in getting a consistent answer. References to *jen* in the *Analects* are somewhat paradoxical. Confucius is depicted as extremely reluctant to ascribe this quality to any given individual. Indeed he expresses doubt that anyone is capable of concentrating his whole effort on humaneness for a single day (A 4.6). This reluctance to admit that anyone attains to *jen* is due to the fact that it is the quality of ideal human nature. On the other hand, since *jen* is an essential ingredient of the human being, not something which depends on anything outside himself, it should in theory be easily attainable, if men were true to their natures. 'Is humaneness really so far away?', he asks. 'If we really wished for it, it would come' (A 7.29). In fact the passage expressing doubt whether anyone was capable of concentrating on humaneness for a single day is directly contradicted by another passage claiming that the Master's favourite disciple Yen Hui was capable of having nothing contrary to humaneness on his mind for three months at a stretch (A 6.5). Although these discrepancies may be due to the composite nature of the work, it is consistent with Confucius's apparent attitudes to suppose that in the case of *jen* there was a difference in the Master's mind between the ideal manifestation of the virtue as attained only in the Golden Age of antiquity and the striving towards it which could be attributed to some of his contemporaries even in the decadent times in which he lived.

Reverence and sensibility as signs of humaneness

Jan Yung asked about humaneness. The Master said: 'When you are away from home, behave as if receiving an important guest. Employ the people as if you were officiating at a great sacrifice. Do not do to others what you would not like yourself. Then there will be no resentment against you, either in the family or in the state.' (A 12.2.)

Tzu-kung said: 'Suppose there were a ruler who benefitted the people far and wide and was capable of bringing salvation to the multitude, what would you think of him? Might he be called humane?' The Master said: 'Why only humane? He would undoubtedly be a sage. Even Yao and Shun would have had to strive to achieve this. Now the humane man, wishing himself to be established, sees that others are established, and wishing himself to be successful, sees that others are successful. To be able to take one's own feelings as a guide may be called the art of humaneness.' (A 6.28)

Despite Confucius's reluctance to apply the label of *jen* to any given individual, these two quotations again show the worldliness and sense of mutual benefit which are at the heart of 'humaneness'. The reply to the disciple Jan Yung (already referred to on p. 29) starts by emphasising the close relationship between *jen* and *li* (ritual). The first ingredient of humaneness is to have an attitude of reverence in human relationships, as if one were taking part in a religious ceremony, or at least to behave with the ceremoniousness and sense of propriety required when receiving an honoured guest. The second ingredient is to show consideration for the feelings of others by not doing to them what you would not like them to do to you, a sentiment which has been compared unfavourably with the golden rule of the Gospels: 'Do ye unto others as ye would that others should do unto you.' The *Analects* has a special term for this ingredient of *jen*, namely *shu*, which is sometimes translated as 'reciprocity'. The passage reveals the same basic element of self-interest in *jen*, which appeared in the reply to Tzu-chang above: if one does not treat others inhumanely, they will not treat one inhumanely in return. In the reply to the disciple Tzu-kung, Confucius again gives a more positive version of the virtue. Both of these sayings maintain that one should take one's own feelings and ambitions as a guide to the desires and needs of others, so that one can treat them with humaneness. The supreme virtue advocated by Confucius is deeply concerned with mutual benefit.

Humane government

'If there existed a true king, after a generation humaneness would certainly prevail.' (A 13.12)

Both of the quotations on p. 40 refer to humaneness as exhibited by a ruler. Obviously humaneness will be more effective and all-embracing when displayed by an ideal sovereign, whose *jen* is such that he is able to protect all the people under his care. *Jen* does not occur very commonly in pre-Confucian texts, but when it does it usually refers to a ruler's kindness towards his subjects. Mencius also, coming after Confucius, was much concerned that rulers should bestow humane government upon their people; and it was the great hope of both thinkers that a true king might arise, a man who had both political power and the necessary kingly qualities, so that through his humaneness he would succeed in converting the whole country to virtuous behaviour. This would be achieved partly by force of example, reinforced with the people's acceptance of the principle that enlightened self-interest leads to the treatment of others as one would like to be treated. But apart from the force of example on human beings, the ruler's act also had cosmic importance. By the performance of the appropriate rituals he could help to secure universal harmony, so that his moral and ritual behaviour had a certain magical quality which could ensure the moral transformation of the people. *Jen* in the ideal sense can only occur as the result of such a complete transformation brought about by the perfect ruler.

The highest political ideal of the Chinese throughout the imperial period was that of an empire presided over by a Son of Heaven who, having received the Mandate of Heaven, ruled as a true king. The ideal is more fully expounded in the teachings of Mencius, but the above quotation, from one of the later chapters and so possibly from a later stratum of the book, does give Confucian authority for the important doctrine of the transforming power of the virtuous ruler. This doctrine had an influence not only in China but also in Europe, where the high ideal of the benevolent despot (rather than the less impressive reality of imperial rule in China) was what greatly impressed Europeans when they first heard of it from the Jesuit missionaries.

All men have equal potentiality for moral growth

'By nature near together; by practice far apart.' (A 17.2)

In considering man's ethical nature the Confucian tradition came up against the question whether human beings were born with equal potentiality for moral growth. Mencius emphatically believed that this was so. He expressed his belief in uncompromising terms: 'Everyone may become a Yao or Shun' (M 6b.2). Coming from a predominantly agricultural society, he conceived of human moral development on the analogy of plant growth. He believed that man's moral personality had four shoots or growth-points, the cultivation of which produced the four basic virtues of humaneness, ritual observance, dutifulness and wisdom. If these young shoots were not properly tended they would wither, but all men were born with an equal capacity for moral development.

It is not easy to say precisely why such an egalitarian philosophy developed in ancient China. Some hold that the belief in natural equality springs from that growth of opposition to hereditary privilege which was characteristic of the late Chou period, but it is hard to see any necessary connection between the two or any evidence from the history of other societies to substantiate this theory. On the other hand a belief in the equality and indeed in the innate goodness of man (a belief which Mencius placed in the forefront of the Confucian tradition) seems a natural corollary of the deeply held Chinese conviction that the universe is a harmony and that mankind is an integral part of that harmony. For Europeans the idea of natural equality is very difficult to accept because they judge in terms of intellectual rather than moral capacity. 'Everyone may become an Einstein' is sheer nonsense, but 'Everyone may become a Yao or Shun' is a hopeful slogan which is not belied by experience.

Although the classical Confucian theory of the equality and goodness of human nature must be attributed to Mencius, the germ of these ideas may be found in the *Analects* by those who really want to find it there. The quotation at the head of this section comes from a book which clearly contains much late material, and it is also very brief and consequently its meaning is uncertain. But in spite of the fact that elsewhere Confucius is reported to have said that men are born with different capacities, distinguishing those who are born with knowledge from those who are not (A 16.9), this passage has been taken to lend Confucian authority to the sentiment that man's differences are due to disparities in education rather than in their nature. This sentiment is then used to support a plea for equal opportunity. The influence of this saying was very powerful because of its prominence as the second couplet in the elementary textbook known as the *Three-Character Classic*, which was committed to memory by many generations of schoolboys. And indeed this simple observation of Confucius was still effective in the mid-twentieth century, when it was accepted as the essential truth with regard to human nature and racial differences by a group of international experts in the UNESCO 'Statement on Race' which was published in July 1950.

The Master's attitude towards ghosts and spirits

Tzu-lu asked about serving ghosts and spirits. The Master said: 'If one is not capable of serving men, how can one serve ghosts?' He ventured to ask about the dead, and the Master said: 'If one does not understand life, how can one understand death?' (A 11.11)

Fan Ch'ih asked about wisdom. The Master said: 'To devote oneself earnestly to securing what is right for the people, and to show reverence for ghosts and spirits so as to keep them at a distance may be called wisdom.' (A 6.20)

The central concern of Confucius was the moral guidance of mankind, and the chief virtue for Confucius was humaneness. Such humanism seems bound to leave less room for concern with ghosts and spirits. If his purpose was to restore a paradise on this earth, there was little room for religion. The reply to Tzu-lu is the *locus classicus* in the *Analects* for the agnosticism and this-worldliness attributed to the Master. It is the main text quoted in support of the argument that Confucianism in general is an agnostic creed, so that the Chinese people have not been burdened with the kind of religious heritage which has sometimes tormented Europe. The most uncompromising critic of religious devotion was in fact Hsün Tzu, who said: 'You pray for rain and it rains. Why? For no particular reason, I say. It is just as though you had not prayed for rain and it rained anyway' (H 85). He thought that sacrifice was totally ineffectual, but merely had social and psychological value. His doctrine that prayer and divination were only taken seriously by the common people, but were viewed by the ruling class as mere manifestations of culture (*wen*), has had a strong influence within the Confucian tradition, and in modern times has particularly appealed to those who have sought to claim superiority for Chinese agnosticism over the turbulent religious tradition of Christianity. But in reality it is plain that Confucius himself did not detach himself from the religious tradition of his people. He shared the common belief in an impersonal Heaven or Providence, which dealt out life and death, wealth and rank (cf. the first quotation on p. 69). He was also regarded as an expert on ritual and sacrifice. 'Sacrifice to the spirits as if the spirits were in one's presence' (A 3.12) was the main theme of his advice. Just as with all ritual, sacrifice must be meaningful and must not lapse into empty ceremony. It must be fresh and sincere, as if the spirits were actually there. The same note is struck in the *Record of Rites*, which says: 'At all sacrifices the bearing and appearance of the worshippers were as if they saw those to whom they were sacrificing' (L 2.26).

The reply to Fan Ch'ih, however, shows the other side of the Chinese reaction to spirits. There has always been an ambivalence, which appears most striking in attitudes towards ancestor-worship. On the one hand there is deep respect for the venerable departed, but on the other hand there is a dark fear of the spirit world, which must be appeased by sacrifice so that it will not harm the living, for hungry ghosts will not let people dwell in peace. Accordingly Confucius talks of the wisdom of keeping the ghosts and spirits at a distance by showing them proper respect.

So although the reply to Tzu-lu does show Confucius giving a remarkably rational priority to this world, this does not mean that the demands of ghosts and spirits could be totally ignored. Although the humanism of Confucius and his followers set its stamp on later Chinese society, China, like all other societies, has been riddled with belief in supernatural intervention in human affairs. This has affected the intellectuals as well as the common people. The great pressure to succeed meant that the civil service examinations were a hotbed of superstitious ideas about success or failure being decided by the intervention of spirits. Scholars' literary functions were often held at the local temple of the God of Literature, and if they succeeded in obtaining a post as district magistrate their official duties included the responsibility of dealing with the city god and other local deities. Among all classes the ancestral spirits and household gods demanded constant attention. Nevertheless the humanism and agnosticism at the core of Confucian belief was reflected in a society in which no church, not even Buddhism at its heyday in the T'ang Dyanasty, ever succeeded in consolidating a powerful and independent position *vis à vis* the state; so that education, for example, always remained a purely secular activity aimed at this-worldly ends.

The late Chou period in general showed much less interest in the world of the spirits than the men of the early Chou period had done. There was much more concern with the problems of men in society. The belief that priority should be given to these problems rather than to the other world, which we can know nothing about, receives its classic formulation in the simple question 'If one does not understand life, how can one understand death?' – yet another of those texts to which the unfolding of Chinese civilisation provides an eloquent sermon.

Filial piety to be shown towards the living and the dead

The Master (on being asked about filial piety) said: 'When they are alive serve them in accordance with ritual; and when they are dead, bury them in accordance with ritual and sacrifice to them in accordance with ritual.' (A 2.5)

'When the father is alive, you only see the son's intentions. It is when he is dead that you see the son's actions. If for three years he makes no change from the ways of his father, he may be called filial.' (A 1.11)

After humaneness, the supreme virtue, it is necessary to consider filial piety, which has already been referred to (together with the twin virtue of brotherly respect) as the root of humaneness. Filial piety consisted of duties towards both the living and the dead. The former aspect included not only obedience to parents but also the responsibility for caring for them and providing food for them in their old age. The latter comprised furnishing a worthy funeral for the dead and offering the proper sacrifices thereafter. These dual responsibilities, and the importance of concern for ritual in carrying them out, are succinctly described in the first quotation. The second quotation epitomises the power of paternal influence over a son's thoughts and actions, which is again typical of Chinese society.

Filial piety, however, is rarely mentioned in the *Analects*, except in the first two books, which may not be part of the oldest stratum of the work. It was certainly the special emphasis laid on family ties by the early Confucians that stimulated Mo Tzu, who was born at about the time of Confucius's death, to become a strong advocate of universal love as opposed to the graded affection he attributed to his antagonists; but in the surviving literature it is the *Book of Filial Piety* – composed probably in the third century BC – that first gives the virtue a pre-eminent position. In that book filial piety is described as the 'root of virtue and the source of all teaching' (Ch. 1). It is again to Confucius that this doctrine is attributed. This first chapter puts into the Master's mouth a description of filial piety which neatly summarises much of what the virtue has stood for in the context of Chinese civilisation. It states that the beginning of filial piety is that one should not dare to harm the physical body which one receives from one's parents, and that the end of filial piety is that one should establish one's character and practise the Way so as to make one's reputation known to later generations and thus bring glory upon one's parents.

So in this work Confucius is represented as the great advocate of a virtue which is of relatively minor interest in the *Analects*, and his opening description of it echoes down the centuries. The *Book of Filial Piety* is presented as a dialogue between the Master and his disciple Tseng Tzu, who was especially famous as a practitioner of this virtue: on his death bed he is said to have ordered that he be stripped naked so that those present could see that he had preseved the perfect body which his parents had given him at birth. He was thus one who observed what the opening chapter of the Classic described as the beginning of filial piety. The 'end of filial piety', the injunction to virtuous conduct in order that the reputation gained thereby might bring glory to the ancestors, had a powerful impact on many generations of Confucian scholars. It stimulated their ambition to study hard to pass the examinations and enter a bureaucratic career, so that their fame might be known to later generations and reflect glory on their parents.

The concept of filial piety was subsequently recognised as an excellent preserver of social stability, for it cemented the family and clan system on which the state depended for order and cohesion. The tensions inherent in the large family which was the Chinese ideal were undoubtedly eased by the need to observe the duties of filial piety and the sense of hierarchy which this virtue produced. Clans had their own published rules of conduct, which stressed filial piety, often quoting the *Analects* or *Book of Filial Piety* in support of their arguments. The legal system, too, was progressively Confucianised during the course of imperial Chinese history, so that it took special account of the duties of filial piety and the rights of a father over his son. Penalties were made more severe if the crime were committed by a son against his father, and conversely the father could deal harshly with his son with impunity. In the late empire the Six Edicts of the Shun-chih emperor (who reigned from 1644 to 1661) and the Sacred Edict of the K'ang-hsi emperor (1661–1722) were collections of commandments which both listed filial piety as the first duty. In order to instil morality into the populace fortnightly lectures were supposed to be delivered by district magistrates, taking these commandments as their texts.

The virtue also had an important influence at the highest level, since it made for extreme conservatism in politics. Respect for the imperial ancestors demanded that emperors retain the institutions handed down to them, and especially those initiated by the dynastic founder, the manifest recipient of the Mandate of Heaven. Filial duty towards the emperor's mother could also have disastrous and far-reaching effects. In the Former Han Dynasty, when the word Filial precedes the title of all the emperors – so that the one known as the Emperor Wu is really the Filial Emperor Wu – these monarchs demonstrated their filial piety by piling high honours onto their mothers' male relatives; and it was through this practice that the dynasty toppled, being superseded by Wang Mang, who owed his power to such a relationship.

Not only filial piety but also the rites of ancestor worship were seen as a means of cultivating moral values among the people. As the disciple Tseng Tzu said, 'Show solicitude for parents at their end and continue this with sacrifices when they are far away, and the people's virtue will be abundantly restored' (A 1.9). The sceptical Hsün Tzu also took the view that ancestor worship was only taken at its face value by the lower orders: 'Among gentlemen it is regarded as a part of the human Way; among the common people it is considered to be the serving of ghosts and spirits' (H 110). The same attitude could be found in the *Record of Rites*, whose authority in these matters was supreme. Sacrifice was 'simply the expression of human feelings'. Its value lay in securing the moral welfare and social harmony of the people.

Among children the doctrine of filial piety was propagated by means of the famous twenty-four examples of that virtue. In keeping with the traditional Chinese idea that education depends on the imitation of models as well as the adoption of rules, children learned the stories of paragons like Wu Meng, who let himself be eaten by mosquitoes in order to divert them from his parents, and Lao Lai-tzu, who in adult life still dressed as a child and played with his toys to make his parents happy. However, the ultimate source of inspiration for filial piety could again be found in words attributed to Confucius, especially in the *Book of Filial Piety* but also in the *Analects*.

Loyalty, and other virtues mentioned in the Analects

Duke Ting asked about a ruler's employment of his ministers, and ministers' service to rulers. Confucius replied: 'A ruler in employing his ministers accords with ritual, and a minister in serving his ruler accords with loyalty.' (A 3.19)

'If one loves people, can one not exact effort from them? If one is loyal to a person, can one not instruct him?' (A 14.8)

Filial piety was the key virtue within the family, but for the Confucian gentleman there was another field of operations, the state. Family and state were often contrasted as 'inside' and 'outside', and it was natural that there should be a virtue which corresponded exactly with filial piety, but was relevant to this wider field of political activity. That virtue was loyalty (*chung*), the duty owed by a minister to his lord and by the people to their ruler. Loyalty is often mentioned in association with good faith (*hsin*), another essential virtue of the political arena, but one which obtains between friends and equals as well as between inferiors and superiors. These virtues were part of everyday social intercourse and were well understood, so Confucius did not need to describe them so much as to advocate them; but in his reply to Duke Ting the Master did make the point that the loyalty of the minister corresponded with the treatment according to ritual which he was supposed to receive from the ruler.

In imperial China the virtue of loyalty was naturally exploited by the autocratic regime. A spurious composition known as the *Book of Loyalty*, a forgery of the late T'ang or early Sung, was widely accepted as a genuine work of antiquity in the Sung and later periods. It was somewhat similar in format to the *Book of Filial Piety* and it taught blind and undeviating loyalty to the ruler. In the later empire, as the state became increasingly despotic, the concept of loyalty became transformed into that of unquestioning subservience, and the support of Confucius himself was claimed for the view that ministers owed absolute loyalty to ruler and dynasty. An ancient hero called Kuan Yü was deified and worshipped as the symbol of loyalty. In the Ch'ing Dynasty he was worshipped in thousands of temples throughout the country, and during the crisis of the middle of the nineteenth century, when the Taiping Rebellion cost millions of lives and almost toppled the dynasty, he was even decreed to be the equal of Confucius. But earlier in the imperial age there had been much more conflict in the minds of scholar-bureaucrats about the nature of loyalty. In antiquity Mencius had set his authority against the unquestioning loyalty of ministers and had strongly proclaimed the duty of ministers to remonstrate with their sovereigns in the interest of wise government; as a consequence remonstrance became not only the right but also the duty of all officials in the Confucian state. Although the reply to Duke Ting might have been used as ammunition by the advocates of blind loyalty, the following quotation attributes the responsibility for admonishing or instructing the object of one's loyalty to Confucius himself. In the *Analects*, *chung* certainly meant 'doing one's best for' rather than blind obedience to the dictates of one's superior.

A short list of the main virtues mentioned in the *Analects* would include humaneness, filial piety, loyalty, good faith, and behaviour in accordance with ritual. Other virtues are mentioned rarely, but have considerable importance in the ethics of Confucianism. There is *shu* (reciprocity – the virtue of not doing to others that which we would not like done to ourselves), and *jang* (deference – the virtue of, for example, the sage monarch who abdicates in favour of another sage). But no complete list of virtues is set out and there is nothing like the four basic virtues of Mencius (humaneness, dutifulness, observance of ritual, and wisdom). The so-called five Confucian virtues (which are these four with the addition of good faith) do not appear as a set in the *Analects* at all, but are a much later categorisation invented by a numerological school of thought which needed to find five virtues to correlate with the five elements and other sets of five.

What all these virtues have in common is that they belong to relationships between human beings, and are all essentially actions rather than states. For us it is possible to conceive of man being virtuous in isolation, to attribute virtue to qualities like calmness and patience which do not necessarily involve positive behaviour towards others. But in the Confucian tradition virtues were not attributes of the recluse. They were to be seen in everyday actions which could be assessed and evaluated. For example, they were used as criteria for evaluating the performance of officials in the civil service. The Confucian virtues still survived in the language of the nineteenth century, when the foreign barbarians were condemned, as ancient rulers had been condemned, because they talked only of profit and had nothing to say about humaneness or filial piety.

There is one virtue of some importance which we have not yet met in the *Analects* and that is *i* (dutifulness), one of the four

Mencian virtues, sometimes also translated as righteousness, rightness, or justice. Its original sense seems to have been natural justice, what seemed just to the natural man before concepts like law and ritual were evolved. In the *Analects* there are only a handful of references to this virtue in the oldest stratum, and it is not specifically mentioned as a topic of Confucius's teaching; but it is clearly regarded as the ultimate yardstick against which matters of law and ritual must be judged. Two things about the use of *i* in the *Analects* stand out: it is treated as the opposite of profit (as in the third quotation on p. 55), and it is regarded as the especial concern of the gentleman, who is the main topic of the chapter which now follows.

5 Gentlemen and knights

The nature of the gentleman

Tzu-lu asked about the gentleman. The Master said: 'He cultivates himself in order to show reverence.' 'Is that all?' asked Tzu-lu. The Master said: 'He cultivates himself so as to bring tranquillity to others.' 'Is that all?', Tzu-lu again asked. The Master said: 'He cultivates himself so as to bring tranquillity to all the people. Even Yao and Shun would have found this a difficult task.' (A 14.45)

Confucius and his followers used various words to describe men of virtue, and the most important of these was *chün-tzu* (gentleman). This passage sets out for posterity the essence of the gentleman's role. The reference to reverence (*ching*) – a word used elsewhere specifically to describe the demeanour which should accompany the performance of ritual (A 3.26) – can be understood by recalling Confucius's insistence that rulers should behave in accordance with ritual when dealing with their ministers (cf. the first quotation on p. 49). But the main message lies in what follows. The gentleman practises self-cultivation, or cultivates his moral personality, in order to bring tranquillity to all men. This puts in a nutshell the Confucian ideal of government: that it is an agency for ensuring that the influence and example of men of superior moral qualities is brought to bear on the population. For the *Analects*, and especially the *Great Learning*, self-cultivation and the ordering of family and society were different aspects of the gentleman's indivisible task; but unfortunately, as Confucius himself discovered, reality did not always permit the deployment of the true gentleman's talents in the political arena. His great tragedy was that he could not find the opportunity in government to match his superior attainments in self-cultivation. He had to content himself with continuing the process of self-cultivation while proclaiming his message about the kind of society in which his ideal of the gentleman, practising self-cultivation and at the same time bringing tranquillity to the people, would be realised. So for Confucian literati down the ages the Master's reply to Tzu-lu provided a description of the ideal role of the gentleman, while his own life served as an inspiration for those who had to adapt the ideal to reality when the times were unfavourable.

The word *chün-tzu*, which is here translated as 'gentleman' and is often rendered as 'superior man', really means 'son of a ruler'; but the meaning extended to include descendants of rulers and then members of the upper class in general. The *chün-tzu* was a gentleman primarily in the class sense, although at the same time he would naturally be expected to follow a code of behaviour appropriate to his rank. Before Confucius the term had always been used to mean gentleman in this primarily social sense, but the Master introduced the idea that social status was irrelevant. A man could be a gentleman without benefit of high birth. So in the *Analects*, as in our own use of 'gentleman', *chün-tzu* implied either superior social status or superior moral accomplishments or both. Since the important task of government was to transform the people through education, and since this involved the study and imitation of models, it followed that Confucius thought of the person in political power, not primarily as a man who could cope skilfully with administrative problems, but as one who would act as an example to the people because of his moral qualities. The gentleman, in Confucius's view, should be one who combined the possession of office with cultivation of his moral personality; and he hoped that men who lacked the advantage of high birth but possessed the moral qualities required of a gentleman could thereby achieve status and play their part in government. Confucius taught a philosophy of government by men serving as moral exemplars rather than government by laws and institutions framed and administered by men.

Further qualities of the gentleman

'If the gentleman is not grave, then he will not inspire awe in others. If he is not learned, then he will not be on firm ground. He should take loyalty and good faith as his first principles, and have no friends who are not up to his own standard. If he commits a fault, he should not shrink from mending his ways.' (A 1.8)

'The gentleman, with his studies broadened by culture and yet restrained by the requirements of ritual, surely cannot overstep the mark.' (A 6.25)

'The gentleman is concerned with what is right, just as the small man is concerned with profit.' (A 4.16)

Some of the qualities which the gentleman must possess are set out in these three quotations. The first begins with a reference to gravity of demeanour, just as the reply to Tzu-lu at the beginning of the chapter commenced with a reference to reverence. This reminds us that behaviour in accordance with ritual is an important responsibility of rulers, and that the appropriate attitude and demeanour are an important aspect of ritual behaviour. The quotation goes on to stress the importance of learning, meaning primarily the moral training necessary for the production of a gentleman, and loyalty and good faith, which are essential components of an aristocratic code of honour. Finally Confucius insists on a willingness to correct faults, which was later also stressed by Mencius, who believed that gentlemen of his day contrasted unfavourably with gentlemen of antiquity, because they did not correct their faults, but instead persisted in them (M 2b.9).

The next quotation makes a contrast between the broadening effect of culture and the restraining influence of ritual, a schematic comparison between these two important components of education which became a commonplace in ancient Chinese literature. Ritual involves a disciplined adherence to rules of conduct, but culture releases man from a life concerned with the mere necessities of existence and exerts a broadening and civilising influence upon him; so the contrast made in this saying is clear enough. The reference to 'studies broadened by culture' gave much food for thought to readers of the *Analects* in late imperial China who fretted against the narrow and sterile intellectual life involved in preparation for the civil service examinations. The saying gave good canonical authority for their disenchantment.

The third of these quotations epitomises the difference between the gentleman and his opposite, the *hsiao jen*, which literally means 'the small man', but is often translated as 'the inferior man' in contrast with 'the superior man', which is sometimes used to translate *chün-tzu*. The gentleman is concerned with what is right or just (*i*), while the small man is concerned only with profit. Lacking moral training, he can only be concerned with his material welfare. Mencius followed Confucius in being very hostile to the profit motive. If a ruler wanted to profit his state, all his subjects would follow his example and strive with each other for profit (M 1a.1). The social class which characteristically pursued profit, that of the merchants and traders, was relegated to the lowest position among the four traditional classes in Chinese society (scholars, farmers, artisans, merchants), so this saying of Confucius not only encapsulates a class distinction based on concern for moral values, but at the same time provides a slogan for that constant subordination of mercantile interests, which has been a distinctive feature of Chinese society.

The rectification of names

'If a gentleman abandons humaneness, how can he fulfil the name?'
(A 4.5)

The gentleman, as the supremely moral man, must set his sights on the supreme virtue of humaneness. The saying indicates that this is implicit in the meaning of the word 'gentleman'. The concept of 'fulfilling the name', i.e. acting completely in accordance with the label one bears, is familiar in ancient Chinese philosophy from the doctrine of the rectification of names (*'cheng ming*). This expression only occurs once in the *Analects* (13.13), where Confucius is reported to have told the disciple Tzu-lu, much to his astonishment, that the rectification of names was the first priority in government. The style of this passage suggests that it is an interpolation dating from the last century of the

Chou Dynasty, when the doctrine of the rectification of names was widely current. Nevertheless the sentiment is certainly present in the *Analects*, even if not formulated as a theory. Confucius was obsessed with the decline from the ancient mores of the early Chou period, with the usurpation of titles and ceremonies, and with the fact that the gentleman (in the class sense) could no longer be trusted to behave as a gentleman (in the moral sense). This is what is implied in the advice the Master gave to Duke Ching of Ch'i when he asked about government: 'Let the prince be a prince, the minister a minister, the father a father, and the son a son' (A 12.11). This was a most appropriate recommendation, since the security of the duke's dynasty was menaced by ministers who were not content to be ministers, and the succession was being squabbled over by sons who were not content to accept their father's authority.

'Rectification of names' is not a very satisfactory term, for it is actualities rather than names which have to be rectified. The doctrine simply means that names originally had firm meanings and that actualities must correspond with them. It is merely another way of referring to the need to return to the Golden Age of the early Chou period, when the implications of the word 'prince' were clearly understood to include duties and responsibilities as well as power, so that princes always acted as princes, which they no longer did in the decadent age in which Confucius lived. If the name 'prince' were rectified, then the prince would always act in a princely fashion, and nobody else would try to usurp his position. As Hsün Tzu explained it, 'When the kings created names, the names were fixed and actualities distinguished from each other. When this principle was carried out so that their intentions were understood, then they were able to guide the people with care and give them unity' (H 140). Hsün Tzu believed that no new words should have been created since they confused the clear-cut correspondence between name and thing laid down in the beginning. Those who were guilty of this crime should be punished in the same way as those who tampered with weights and measures. The Legalists, whose ideology toughened the sinews of the all-conquering Ch'in state in the late Chou period, also made use of this theory. They thought that, if names could be made to correspond exactly with the responsibilities they implied, this would be an aid towards the impersonal system of administration they wished to introduce. This depended on the automatic implementation of laws and regulations without any discretion being left to human judgement – the exact opposite of Confucian reliance on government by morally qualified human beings.

The idea that in the beginning there was a planned correspondence between things and the names given to them is obviously more credible to people who write with a script which was pictographic in origin. But the doctrine as universalised by Hsün Tzu and the Legalists seems naïve and bizarre. For Confucius the rectification of names was not meant to apply to all names. He merely wanted princes and ministers and others with moral responsibilities to live up to the full meaning of those terms, as had happened at the beginning of the Chou Dynasty; and in this sense the Master's alleged claim that the rectification of names is the first priority in government, although occurring in what is apparently a late interpolation in the text, is not in conflict with the rest of his philosophy as we understand it from the *Analects*.

The gentleman is not a specialist, but a leader

'A gentleman is not an implement.' (A 2.12)

This saying sums up the idea that the gentleman's training should not be confined to particular skills so that he may become the tool or implement of others. It must instead develop his moral qualities and powers of leadership. In a passage in the *Analects* Confucius himself is accused of having many special skills, but he exculpates himself on the grounds that youthful poverty made it necessary for him to earn his living (A 9.6). Confucius also continued to be treated as a specialist on ritual, but this was tolerable since it was not a mere matter of technical knowledge. It was one of the six arts of the traditional education and was closely associated with morality. Of course the conventional education of the well-born young man included not only ritual but such practical accomplishments as archery and charioteering, but the Confucian literature in general regards those who have special skills as inferior to those who have the moral qualities appropriate to the leadership and organisation of these lesser talents. Hsün Tzu put the case for the generalist against the specialist very clearly:

The farmer is skilled in agriculture, but he cannot do the job of a supervisor of agriculture. The merchant is skilled in marketing, but he cannot do the job of a supervisor of markets. The artisan is skilled in craftsmanship, but he cannot do the job of a supervisor of crafts. But there are men who, although they are incapable of these three skills, may be employed to fill these three supervisory posts. This is because they are skilled in the Way. (H 130)

This philosophy obviously suited a class which could depend on the labour of others, and it became crystallised in the imperial civil service examination system, which was designed to recruit for the service of the state people who had had the training for moral and political leadership which was thought to derive from an intensive study of the Classics. The result was that many generations of bureaucrats in China received an education which, although it sometimes included more practical elements like law, was dominated by classical literature. In more modern times the efficacy of an education in self-cultivation and the niceties of ritual may have been called in question because of its inappropriateness for dealing with the specialised problems of a society more complicated than that of ancient China. It could nevertheless be argued that the kind of problems with which bureaucrats had to deal required a basic understanding of human nature and of the ethical relationships between human beings, and demanded the application to concrete situations of general principles derived from the country's cultural heritage, rather than the kind of specialist knowledge which could, when needed, be supplied by underlings. Certainly the idea that gentlemen should be generalists who do not get their hands dirty is very deep-rooted in China and has proved very durable even in the face of persistent Communist attempts to break down class barriers. The saying 'The gentleman is not an implement' is the classic Confucian expression of this ideal.

Gentlemen do not form parties

'Gentlemen are proud but not quarrelsome. They are sociable, but do not form parties.' (A 15.21)

In *chün-tzu pu tang*, 'Gentlemen are not partisan, do not form parties', *tang* is the word which is used in modern times for political parties, as in Kuomintang. The meaning of the original is not clear, since in the *Analects* and the *Mencius tang* normally means a village. However, it does mean 'partisan' or 'party' in other ancient texts as well as in modern usage; and so, interpreted in this sense, this is another of the slogans taken from the *Analects* which must have had a powerful effect on bureaucratic attitudes. The role of ministers in ancient China was conditioned by the model of the individual wise man giving advice to the ruler, who listened and then decided the issue on the basis of that advice; indeed the word *ting*, meaning 'to listen', was often used in the sense of 'to govern'. The forming of parties or factions was likely to be interpreted as a means of pushing the interests of an individual, of espousing the cause of a younger son against the claim of an heir apparent, or even of attempting to overthrow the regime. Similarly in imperial China officials had the right and indeed the duty to remonstrate as individuals, and criticism of the regime was also channeled through the institution of the Censorate; which enabled the Censors, again as individuals, to remonstrate with the ruler. In the bureaucracy at large the formation of factions was suspect because it conflicted with the holistic conception of political organisation. Ties of kinship and of friendship between former fellow-students provided forms of association more congenial to Confucian ideology, and these had some influence in the political arena, though for the purpose of securing personal advancement rather than the achievement of purely political ends. Any such establishment of parties for political purposes was generally thought of as a disruptive element in political life. Factionalism was a dirty word, and not a proper occupation for gentlemen, as Confucius himself had indicated.

The qualities of the knight

'A knight whose heart is set on the Way, but who is ashamed of bad clothes and bad food, is not fit to be consulted.' (A 4.9)

Tzu-kung asked: 'What must a man be like to be called a knight?' The Master said: 'One who in conducting himself maintains a sense of honour, and who when sent to the four quarters of the world does not disgrace his prince's commission, may be called a knight.' (A 13.20)

'The determined knight and the humane man never seek life at the expense of injuring humaneness. They will even sacrifice their lives in order to achieve humaneness.' (A 15.8)

Between the gentleman (*chün-tzu*) and the common people there was another class known as the *shih*, which Arthur Waley translated as 'knight'. This class consisted of the younger sons of aristocrats, who had no opportunities of holding hereditary office, together with the descendants of ruling families who were dispossessed when their states were wiped out during this period of history, in which the large states continued to eliminate their smaller neighbours. They served as officers in time of war and held administrative positions in time of peace. They were schooled in the six arts of the traditional education; and therefore, in addition to military skills, they had the literacy and numeracy and knowledge of ritual which made them a reservoir of talent available at a time when promotion increasingly went to the meritorious. The society of the late Chou period was not only more egalitarian, but also increasingly complex and therefore in greater need of the specialist skills which the *shih* class had to offer. Their talent and ambition continued to stimulate the process of change from hereditary rule to meritocracy.

Confucius himself was a member of this class, and he provided the training necessary for other members of it as well as people of humbler birth to fit themselves for work in government; but in conformity with the rest of his philosophy he insisted on the moral implications of knighthood, so the simple code of loyalty and good faith which the *shih* observed in pre-Confucian times was broadened and given new moral content by the Master and his disciples. A careful study of the *Analects* lends support to the view that this development did not reach its climax until after Confucius's time, for in that book the word *shih* occurs surprisingly rarely, and there is only one instance in the supposedly earliest stratum of the book in which the word is put into the mouth of the Master himself – the first of the quotations given above.

Here in these few references we see some of the essential qualities of the knight. He is oblivious to comfort, as Confucius himself was. Mencius also emphasised this characteristic by saying that it was only the knight who was capable of maintaining a constant heart without having a constant livelihood (M 1a.7). Secondly, in employment in the affairs of state he must be the true counterpart of the morally excellent gentleman who employs him. And, thirdly, he must also be a defender of the supreme virtue of humaneness even at the cost of his life. This call to martyrdom was taken seriously by many generations of Confucian scholar-bureaucrats. Some gave their lives for daring to criticise their rulers. A famous case of a man who courted martyrdom was Han Yü, the literary giant of the T'ang Dynasty, who bitterly attacked the emperor's veneration of a Buddhist relic. Fortunately he was saved from paying the ultimate penalty by the intervention of powerful friends. He was banished to a remote and unhealthy part of the country, where he could bear his exile with fortitude in the knowledge that he had kept faith with the Confucian Way.

In the long run the word *shih*, which had originally implied military status rather than civil accomplishment, came to be used as the name for one of the four classes in Chinese society in addition to farmers, artisans and merchants. In this sense it meant the scholar-bureaucrat ruling class. So the Confucian writings, in establishing a code of conduct for the new administrative middle class known as *shih*, at the same time provided a code for the ruling scholar-bureaucrat class in imperial China, because they were also known as *shih*. Because of its later usage the word *shih* in ancient texts has frequently been mistranslated as 'scholar', for example in James Legge's version of the *Analects*. But the *shih* of the *Analects* is still very much the man of action, the knight whose heart is set on the Way and who is willing to sacrifice his life for humaneness.

6 Government and people

Governments must have the confidence of the people

Tzu-kung asked about government. The Master said: 'Enough food, enough weapons, and the confidence of the people.' Tzu-kung said: 'Suppose you definitely had no alternative but to give up one of these three, which would you relinquish first?' The Master said: 'Weapons.' Tzu-kung said: 'Suppose you definitely had no alternative but to give up one of the remaining two, which would you relinquish first?' The Master said: 'Food. From of old death has come to all men, but a people without confidence in its rulers will not stand.' (A 12.7)

The response to moral and humane government by gentlemen (*chün-tzu*) and knights (*shih*) will be the respect, loyalty, and confidence of the people. The supreme importance of winning the confidence of the people is expressed in this striking reply to the disciple Tzu-kung. The political importance of the people was not a new idea. In the *Book of History* we read: 'Heaven sees and hears as the people see and hear'; and the doctrine of the Mandate of Heaven justified rebellion to get rid of a tyrannical ruler. Confucius himself had nothing to say about the confidence of the people being won by actually consulting them and taking their opinion into account, but Mencius went so far as to say that the views of the people should be canvassed concerning cases of promotion, dismissal, or crimes meriting the death penalty (M 1b.7). So government for the people and in consultation with the people was a basic Confucian ideal, but the further step of government by the people was never an issue in traditional China.

The original strength of this doctrine clearly derived from the political situation in late Chou China, when the contending states needed to attract larger populations to help build up their military power. Unlike their contemporaries in Greece, who went off to find new territories overseas and colonise them, the Chinese states of the time had plenty of undeveloped land for their peasants to exploit; so, in the opinion of Mencius, the way to attract a sufficient population was to win the confidence of the people by a humane government which saw to it that their interests were consulted. This theme remained a powerful one in Chinese history, not only in the hearts of political idealists, but also in the more pragmatic calculations of governments, which constantly tried to maintain the confidence of the people by demonstrating that the regime had supernatural help and therefore obviously retained the Mandate of Heaven. At the local level, too, the task of maintaining peace by suppressing bandits was thought to depend much on considering the people's welfare so that they would extend their loyalty to the officials rather than collaborate with the anti-government forces. In the twentieth century the Communist victory could be seen as a triumph for the belief that a small and isolated force suffering from a serious shortage of both food and weapons, could eventually triumph through winning the minds of the people, a striking confirmation of the fact that Confucius had got his priorities right. The idea that the state was a co-operative enterprise, not a business run for the benefit of the rulers, was deeply rooted in the Confucian tradition.

The people must be properly instructed

'The people may be made to follow it, but may not be made to understand it.' (A 8.9)

Chi K'ang-tzu asked Confucius about government, saying: 'Suppose I were to kill those who lack the Way in order to advance those who have the Way, would that be all right?' Confucius replied: 'You are running the government, so what is the point of killing? If you desire good, the people will be good. The nature of the gentleman is like the wind, and the nature of the small people is like the grass. When the wind blows over the grass it always bends.' (A 12.19)

'Only when good men have instructed the people for seven years, may they take up arms. . . . To lead an uninstructed people into battle may be described as throwing them away.' (A 13.29 and 30)

In Mencius's view consultation with the people was possible, and indeed necessary for the sake of political harmony; but the further step of government by the people is incompatible with the Confucian idea that men have distinct roles which they must perform for the sake of the orderly arrangement of society ('Let the prince be a prince, the minister a minister, the father a father, and the son a son'). It is in direct conflict with the idea that the prerequisite for the restoration of the Golden Age is the rectification of names so that all these roles are properly performed. In the Confucian philosophy government has to be the function of a specialist ruling group.

As compared with Mencius who, reflecting the social turmoil of a later era, envisaged a more active role for the people, Confucius still looked upon them as a largely passive force. Although the winning of their confidence was essential to government, they were to be moulded and influenced rather than consulted. This is the idea behind the first saying above, which has caused some anxiety among defenders of Confucius, since it apparently takes too dismissive an attitude towards the people, who in theory are generally capable of moral understanding if presented with virtuous models to follow. But obviously the gentleman, who has the advantage of a thorough education, will have a level of moral understanding which is denied to the ordinary people, who cannot be expected to have the requisite vision and must take things on trust.

The reply to Chi K'ang-tzu, the usurper who was acting as dictator of Lu, contains the famous simile of the wind and the grass, which was also used by Mencius and became a cliché in later literature. Taken out of context it might be thought to mean that the people always gave way to the gentleman or were beaten down by him; but, as the context makes clear, it illustrates the familiar theme of the powerful moral influence which the gentleman exerts on the people.

The morale of the people and their confidence in their rulers were regarded as the most vital factor in warfare, as we have already seen. Therefore the people must not be used in battle unless they have been subjected to the kind of training in moral values which will prepare them for the fray. This is not just philosophical fantasy. In the historical writings also there are references to the people being trained in the virtues of good faith, dutifulness, and behaviour in accordance with ritual before they are thought fit to go into action. The fact that government was thought of as a matter of instruction and example is clearly demonstrated in the above three quotations.

Government is a matter of setting a moral example

Chi K'ang-tzu asked about inducing the people to be respectful and loyal so that they might be encouraged to support him. The Master said: 'If you approach them with dignity, they will respect you. If you are dutiful towards your parents and kind to your children, then they will be loyal. If you promote the good and instruct the incompetent, then they will be encouraged.' (A 2.20)

Someone said to Confucius: ' Why do you not take part in government?' The Master said: 'What does the *Book of History* say about filial piety? "Only be dutiful towards your parents and friendly towards your brothers, and you will be contributing to government." These virtues also constitute taking part in government.' (A 2.21)

Chi K'ang-tzu asked Confucius about government. Confucius replied saying: 'To govern means to rectify. If you were to lead the people by means of rectification, who would dare not to be rectified?' (A 12.17)

The first of these three quotations shows how the moral example of the ruler is expected to be reciprocated by the people. Government was largely a matter of operating in the wider context of the state with virtues which were really more appropriate within the narrower context of the family. The ruler must practise filial piety and then his subjects will practise the parallel virtue of loyalty towards him. He must instruct and encourage his subjects as a father instructs and encourages his children. The saying also mentions promotion on merit, a common theme in the late Chou period when there was general hostility towards the old system of hereditary office.

The second quotation gives consolation to those who have no political power by saying that the practice of social virtues within the family must itself make a real contribution to government, since it is contributing to the social harmony which is the purpose of government. So this is the Confucian version of the people's participation in government: they respond to examples sent down from above and contribute to the order of the state by securing harmony within the family, one of the microcosmic units of which the macrocosm of the state is composed. As we saw earlier, this Confucian message was used by imperial governments for the purpose of political control. If clans had their own moral codes and were largely capable of policing themselves, the task of the government in trying to secure civil order was made much easier. From the state's point of view it was convenient if the people contributed to stability and harmony by contentedly practising the constant norms of human behaviour within their families. The precepts of Confucius about government often seem appropriate only to a small and cosy community, and it is remarkable that they should have provided the ideology of an enormous bureaucratic state. This could only happen because of the age-old dogma that the state was the family writ large, and the belief that the family virtues were a structural part of the cosmic order.

Finally, the reply to Chi K'ang-tzu depends on the fact that the words for 'to govern' and 'to rectify' were etymologically related to each other. The task of government was to rectify society and so restore it to ancient virtues. The same word is used in the expression *cheng ming*, 'the rectification of names'. This emphasis on rectification remained a keynote of Chinese political thought, so that political reform has generally been seen as rectification rather than innovation. It has generally been regarded as an attempt to get back to ancient wisdoms and ancient ways, and to understand the teaching of the ancients more clearly and restore society to the norms that they laid down.

Miscellaneous advice on government

'To lead a country of a thousand chariots, the ruler must attend reverentially to business and be of good faith. He must practise economy in expenditure and love all men, and employ the people in accordance with the seasons.' (A 1.5)

Much other miscellaneous advice on government is given in the

Analects, and this passage is included here as a good example of the difficulty of evaluating the book, for it is an amalgam of ideas more readily associated with other texts. 'Economy in expenditure' is the name of a section of the *Mo Tzu*, in which that philosopher takes a most utilitarian view of production, and will not allow anything decorative in the manufacture of clothing, houses, weapons, boats, or vehicles, an argument which is out of sympathy with Confucian support of culture (*wen*). The love of all men equally was also advocated by Mo Tzu in opposition to the graded love, giving preference to the claims of kinship, which he regarded as characteristic of Confucianism. Finally the employment of the people in accordance with the seasons was a favourite theme of Mencius, who criticised rulers for switching the peasants from their agricultural labours to the provision of luxuries for their palaces. On the other hand, the Mohist school soon faded into oblivion, and the two Mohist principles included in this saying are not in the long run inimical to Confucianism. The frugality suggested by the words 'economy in expenditure', the pursuit of ideals despite a life of hardship, was regarded as a virtue by Confucius. And, despite Mo Tzu's criticism of the graded love associated with Confucianism, the love of all men is inherent in the Confucian notion of humaneness, which, if displayed by a ruler, is capable of protecting all within the Four Seas.

All men are brothers: even barbarians can learn from example

'Other men all have brothers,' said Ssu-ma Niu in his distress, 'but I alone have none.' Tzu-hsia said: 'I have heard that death and life are predestined, and riches and honours depend on Heaven. If a gentleman is reverent and avoids error, if he is courteous with others and observes the obligations of ritual, then all within the Four Seas are his brothers. Why should a gentleman be distressed at having no brothers?' (A 12.5)

The Master wished to dwell among the nine wild tribes of the East. Someone said: 'They are uncivilised, so what will you do about that?' The Master said: 'If a gentleman dwelt among them, what lack of civility would they show?' (A 9.13)

Ssu-ma Niu's anxiety is said to have stemmed from the fact that his brother could no longer be regarded as a brother because he had attempted to kill Confucius. The reply is put into the mouth of the disciple Tzu-hsia, but the commentators claim without any evidence at all that it was from Confucius that he had heard the saying. Consequently the famous tag 'All within the Four Seas are brothers' is taken out of context and attributed to Confucius. The ancient Chinese believed that the inhabited world was surrounded on all four sides by oceans, which encompassed not only the Chinese people themselves but also those whom they recognised as culturally distinct. The idea that all within the Four Seas are brothers states dramatically what is implicit in Confucius's concept of the virtue of humaneness. The further implication is that in the long run the whole of the inhabited world is ideally and potentially subject to the one political regime administered by the moral and ritual-conscious Confucian gentleman. This then is the high-minded theory behind Confucian attitudes to barbarians. It is just a question of time before all are absorbed into the Chinese world as a result of the transforming power of Confucian virtue.

The passage referring to Confucius's desire to live among the eastern barbarians puts plainly this idea that a Confucian gentleman only has to go and dwell among foreigners for them to be affected by the transforming power of his virtue. As explained before, the difference between the Chinese and barbarians was seen as cultural rather than racial. Among the peoples which inhabited this part of the world there were no striking racial distinctions in physical appearance, so it was those people who had not absorbed Chinese culture who were thought of as alien. After the upsurge of Confucianism during the reign of Emperor Wu of the Former Han Dynasty, who was on the throne from 140 to 87 BC, local officials were trained in Confucian studies. As the empire extended to embrace barbarian areas in the South, these officials, inspired with the aim of transforming the people in accordance with Confucian ideals, not only introduced improved agricultural technology to enable them to provide themselves with an adequate livelihood (without which, according to Mencius, they could not be expected to lead virtuous lives), but also gave the ignorant natives the blessing of instruction in filial piety itself, introducing the concept of marriage to people who were unfamiliar with the whole idea, so that for the first time men began to know who their fathers were.

The inspiration for all these arduous activities among remote peoples living in appalling climates lay in the words of Confucius and Mencius. The latter, as often, pushed the argument a stage further than Confucius, for he spoke of barbarians positively clamouring for their domains to be conquered by the exemplary King T'ang, founder of the Shang Dynasty (M 1b.11). Mencius's attitude suggests that the Confucian's duty was a crusade to liberate the barbarian peoples from their oppressive rulers. But the ultimate model was the quieter example of Confucius, who was supremely confident that, by living according to the prescriptions of ritual and ethics, one gentleman would be able by his mere presence to convert the barbarians from their coarse, untutored ways.

The Master's antipathy to litigation

'At hearing legal proceedings I am just like anybody else, but what is necessary is to bring it about that there is no litigation.' (A 12.13)

A further indicator of the importance attached by the Confucians to government by virtuous example is their very negative attitude to litigation. They felt that, if everyone observed the moral code, there would be no need to invoke the processes of law. Confucian belief in the emulation of virtuous models came into direct conflict with the Legalists, who believed that it was necessary to control people through fear of punishments. The Confucian attitude is seen not only in the philosophical writings but also in the *Tso Tradition*, the main historical source for the period, where it is reported that in 513 BC, when the state of Cheng cast bronze vessels on which were inscribed a code of penal laws, Confucius was critical. He argued that 'the people will study the vessels and not care to honour their men of rank. But when there is no distinction of noble and mean, how can a state continue to exist?' This is a classic statement of the Confucian belief that a hierarchical society is essential to the achievement of political order. It sounds like the sort of thing that Hsün Tzu might have said, put into the mouth of Confucius to give it greater weight.

The most important argument against controlling the people by penal law was as set out in this saying attributed to Confucius: universally applied laws would militate against the natural distinction in society between noble and base. The second argument was that, since laws cannot take all possible circumstances into account, it is better to leave matters to the judgement of morally qualified persons rather than to the mechanical application of a legal code. The third argument was that law merely controls through fear of punishment and does not play any part in the moulding of character. It does not educate, or rectify, or make any contribution towards the Confucian aim of transforming the people, as does the emulation of virtuous models. In Europe law has had a fairly good name, but in China, where it had no divine sanction and was thought of as man-made, arbitrary, and inferior to the requirements of ritual, it had a bad name, which became worse when the hated Legalists – literally the 'School of Law' – provided the inspiration for the ruthless Ch'in Dynasty, which caused much suffering to the people in its attempt at rapidly consolidating the unification of China in the late third century BC.

Quite apart from ideological considerations, the Confucians, who were the experts on ritual, had a vested interest in ensuring that its role in providing rules for society was not entirely taken away by law. Inevitably, however, the need for law increased, since a great empire cannot be administered without a complex and pervasive legal system. It may seem therefore that this was one battle that the Confucians lost to the Legalists, but in fact in imperial China the law took on a distinctly Confucian complexion. Not only did it fix a scale of penalties which varied according to the relationship between the perpetrator and the victim of the crime; it was also much influenced by the principle set out in the *Record of Rites* to the effect that the code of ritual was appropriate for the gentleman and law should apply only to the common people (L 1.90). Throughout imperial Chinese history officials, whether active or retired, enjoyed a very privileged position in matters of law, a distinction ultimately deriving from the idea that the educated man's sense of honour should be sufficient to ensure that he conforms with the demands of *li* and does not need to be controlled by fear of punishment.

The ancient debate between the opposing ideals of the rule of law and rule by good men continued right through to the nineteenth century. The hostility to litigation which Confucius had expressed continued to be a characteristic of Chinese society. It was often featured in clan rules, perhaps less out of good Confucian principle than because of a vivid awareness that the harshness of the state's legal processes was exacerbated by the extortionate behaviour of the police and other underlings, so that it was much better to settle matters without recourse to the law.

The people should be led by virtue rather than by fear

'If you lead the people by means of regulations and keep order among them by means of punishments, they will be without conscience in trying to avoid them. If you lead them by virtue and keep order among them by ritual, they will have a conscience and will reform themselves.' (A 2.3)

'He who rules by means of virtue may be compared to the pole-star, which keeps its place while all the other stars pay homage to it.' (A 2.1)

The first of these two quotations again contrasts ritual with law, and argues that punishments inflicted in accordance with the law do not have the capacity to give people the conscience and sense of morality which will make them obedient to the ruler's wishes. It also contrasts 'regulations' with the word *te*, which I have translated as 'virtue'. This is an extremely important concept in ancient Chinese thought. It is the word that occurs in the title of the Taoist classic *Tao Te Ching*, which Arthur Waley translated as *The Way and its Power*. 'Moral power' or 'moral influence' may often be a more appropriate translation, but the advantage of the word 'virtue' is that, like *te*, it does denote inherent nature or quality as well as moral excellence. *Te*, like virtue, can be used in contexts in which it has nothing to do with morality, as for example in the second quotation on page 65, where it is used to mean 'nature' in 'the nature of the gentleman is like the wind'. The difficulty of retaining it as the translation of this word in all circumstances is that it can be misleading since *te* does not mean virtue as contrasted with vice, for this polarity was alien to the thought-patterns of the ancient Chinese, who conceived of the universe as a kind of harmonious structure. This structure could break down, but there was no room in the concept for vice as a positive element.

The word *te* has played a very important part in Confucian political theory. At the beginning of its reign a dynasty was thought to have an abundant store of virtue or moral influence as a corollary of the fact that it had been entrusted with the Mandate of Heaven. Referring to the days of King Wen, Confucius said that the *te* of Chou could be described as perfect (A 8.20). This stock of *te* would decline as the dynasty deteriorated from its early excellence and lost the moral qualities which had won it the Mandate. In the first quotation *te* is used in contrast with regulations, but often it is used in opposition to *li*, meaning 'force' (a different character from *li* 'ritual'). In Mencius's schematic philosophy the men who ruled by force were the *pa* or paramount princes who became the *de facto* leaders of the Chinese world. Mencius abhorred them because they wielded authority which properly belonged to the Chou rulers, who were now too weak to exert more than a purely symbolical leadership. He contrasted the *pa* with the *wang* or true king, who did not rule by force but by his virtue or moral power (*te*). Rule by *te* rather than by force was traditionally thought to be the means to secure the allegiance of the barbarian peoples on China's frontiers, so later on in Chinese history it was very difficult to explain why the highly civilised Sung were conquered by the barbarous Mongols. The quotation also shows the close relationship between *te* and *li* (ritual): the inherent virtue of the ruler would be manifested in the appropriate ritual behaviour.

The second quotation seems to suggest that Confucius himself believed that the virtuous ruler had a kind of cosmic role. This idea is not fully set out in the *Analects*, but later theory held that the ruler, governing by means of virtue, secured harmony not only in the human world, but also in the cosmos. Throughout imperial Chinese history it was the belief that the virtuous conduct of the emperor at the apex of human society was necessary in order to ensure the smooth operation of nature. If he contravened the dictates of ritual and neglected the requirements of virtuous government, natural calamaties were bound to ensue. The comparison with the pole-star also contains a flavour of the idea of rule by inactivity, the belief that, if a ruler's *te* or moral power were sufficiently great, government would run so smoothly that he would not need to take any action. But this is a fundamentally Taoist notion, which occurs in more blatant form in A 15.4, where the legendary sage-emperor Shun is said to have ruled by the Taoist principle of non-action, merely placing himself reverently with his face to the south and doing nothing. Such a concept is alien to the philosophy of the *Analects* and of Confucianism in general and should therefore be discounted in evaluations of Confucius's thought. According to the Confucian teachings, activity meant to benefit others is an essential part of virtue.

Men's lives should conform with the Way

'Be of unwavering good faith and love learning. Be steadfast unto death in pursuit of the good Way. Do not enter a state which is in peril, nor reside in one in which the people have rebelled. When the Way prevails in the world, then show yourself. When it does not, then hide. When the Way prevails in your own state, to be poor and obscure is a disgrace; but when the Way does not prevail in your own state, to be rich and honoured is a disgrace.' (A 8.13)

'Riches and honours are what men desire, but if this cannot be achieved in accordance with the Way, I do not cling to them. Poverty and obscurity are what men hate, but if this cannot be achieved in accordance with the Way, I do not avoid them.' (A 4.5)

'What I call a great minister serves his ruler in accordance with the Way, and when it is impossible to do so he resigns.' (A 11.23)

'In the morning, hear the Way; in the evening die content!' (A 4.8)

An ideal ethico-political system such as Confucius believed to have existed in the early part of the Chou Dynasty is known as the Way (*Tao*). *Tao* is a very important word in ancient Chinese literature. It is the key concept in the philosophy of Taoism, but in that context it is the Way of Nature, a much broader and more metaphysical notion than the this-worldly Way of Confucius, the Way of running a state so that good order and harmony can prevail among men. *Tao* literally means a path or road, and this literal sense is still present in the words attributed to Tseng Tzu: 'The knight must be broad-shouldered and stout of heart. His burden is heavy and his *way* is long. For humaneness is the burden he has taken upon himself; is it not true that it is a heavy one to bear? Only with death does his journey end; is it not true that he has far to go?' (A 8.7). In the metaphorical and philosophical sense of Way there are really two distinct usages. Sometimes it seems to be regarded as something which existed in remote antiquity and is now almost unattainable, but other passages accept the possibility of the Way existing in the present decadent age. The final brief quotation is an example of the former usage: it suggests that to comprehend the Way is such a sublime experience that it would be worth having even if death immediately followed. On the other hand the first two quotations suggest that some kind of harmonious political order is sometimes achieved, and so in a sense the Way does sometimes prevail even in this imperfect world.

These two senses of Way reflect a conflict at the heart of Confucianism, between the belief that true fulfilment for the gentleman lay in political activity, and the frequent experience that the world was not a fit place for him to deploy his talents in. However deplorable the political situation in the state of Lu and however dark the prospect of improvement, Confucius was training his disciples to hold office. Several of them did achieve positions in government, and he would have been glad to obtain employment himself so that he could try to get his ideals accepted. Sometimes he is depicted as showing great distress at not finding scope for his talents. 'Am I a bitter gourd,' he cried, 'fit to hang up but not to eat?' (A 17.7). Talent he regarded as a precious object, which should not be kept hidden away; and when the disciple Tzu-kung asked: 'Suppose one has a beautiful jade, should one wrap it up, put it in a box, and keep it, or try to get a good price and sell it?', the Master said: 'Sell it indeed! Sell it! I too am one who is waiting for an offer' (A 9.12). One should be involved in the political world, and one should indeed even be prepared to die for the good Way, as the first of the above quotations says, just as one should be prepared to die for humaneness (cf. the last quotation on p. 61). And if the Way does prevail, it is quite acceptable to be rich and honoured. Indeed it is a positive disgrace to be obscure in such circumstances.

The dilemma for good Confucians would always be that one must take office to help realise the Way, but one must not, by staying in office, compromise one's commitment to the Way. The duty of resignation if the Way does not prevail is equally compelling, and the third quotation is an uncompromising message to countless generations of Confucians wondering whether they could reconcile service with their Confucian consciences. Renunciation of office and of political ambition was no easy step since participation in government was the goal of all educated men. Indeed renunciation of official life was regarded by the Chinese as a form of eccentricity comparable with being a hermit in other cultures. But, if divorced from political life, a man could still pursue his commitment to the Way by practising self-cultivation and finding scope for the exercise of his virtues within the family and the local community, reflecting that the frustration of not being employed in affairs of state had once been endured by the Master himself.

The alternative to the Way is disorder. The attainment of the Way is essentially the attainment of harmony. Therefore states which enjoyed a period of relative tranquillity might be described as having the *Tao*, even if it were not the *Tao* of the ancients. *Tao* resembles *jen* (humaneness) in that, despite its being – in its perfect form – something which belonged only to the Golden Age of antiquity and was therefore almost beyond hope of attainment, it was – in the sense of being the natural state of humanity – easily attainable or at any rate the most obvious goal. Just as Confucius said: 'Is humaneness really so far away? If we really wished for it, it would come' (A 7.29), so in the case of *Tao* he said: 'Who can go out without using the door? So why does nobody follow the Way?' (A 6.15). Confucius believed that the universe was characterised by order, and that it was possible for human beings to understand that order.

Confucius does not ever define what he means by *Tao*. It is not anything which can be defined. It is a model of political order which can be best understood by studying the Way of the ancients, a model to be studied and followed just as moral training consisted of the study and imitation of model individuals. It meant a society in which all the highest moral and political ideas were followed. To devote oneself to the study of the Way and to attempt to bring it into being for one's own generation was the highest calling of the gentleman.

7 A Confucian China

Throughout this book I have, as a matter of convenience, frequently referred to the sayings or doctrines of Confucius when it would have been more accurate, although more clumsy, to have written of the sayings and doctrines 'attributed to Confucius in the *Analects*'. In the introductory chapter I maintained that it was difficult to write a book about the Master because of the lack of reliable knowledge about the man and his teachings. It was impossible to be sure that Confucius actually made any of the remarks attributed to him. The men who wrote about him either idolised him or tried to claim his support for doctrines which did not belong to him. Even the *Analects* showed much evidence of later additions; and, even in the apparently more authentic parts, the material was extremely sketchy, consisting largely of brief pronouncements rather than reasoned argument in support of a philosophical system.

My method of dealing with this unpromising situation was to point out that the importance of Confucius for China consists precisely in the transmission of these brief tags, since they have served as slogans for the guidance of Chinese social and political life throughout the ages. In these circumstances what the Western reader with no great knowledge of Chinese civilisation needed to be shown was, not simply what these often mysterious sayings had meant in the context of the China of the later Chou Dynasty, but also how they provided inspiration for Chinese institutions and attitudes right through until the present century. Just as in the Maoist era the sayings of the Chairman were reference points for policy decisions, so in imperial China the sayings of Confucius were often the ultimate authority in all spheres of social and political life.

Nevertheless, after treating the subject as concretely as possible by focusing attention on the significance of individual sayings, it is possible and desirable to summarise the message of the book by means of a general survey of the influence of Confucius (or rather of the sayings and writings associated with his name) on Chinese civilisation.

This influence may be observed firstly in the field of education. His name was closely linked with all the works in the canon of Five Classics set at the forefront of the educational system in the Former Han Dynasty. This was the culmination of a sequence of events which now needs to be described. After the Master's death a Confucian school gradually grew in strength as the disciples preserved and transmitted his teachings and other major figures like Mencius and Hsün Tzu added their contributions to the tradition; but Confucianism was only one of the so-called Hundred Schools which flourished during an age when it became fashionable for rulers to patronise well-known men of learning and gather them together to discuss matters of morals and politics at their courts. All this freedom of thought was swept away when the state of Ch'in triumphed and unified China. In 213 BC the new dynasty staged the execrated 'burning of the books', which was intended to remove from circulation the writings of the philosophical schools antagonistic to the state-sponsored Legalism, and indeed all literature apart from the historical records of Ch'in and books on certain practical subjects. Although copies of the banned works were preserved in the palace library for the benefit of the regime's own scholars, these also perished in the great conflagration which accompanied the downfall of the dynasty.

Eventually much of the older literature was recovered and restored, but only Confucianism and Taoism had the resilience to survive and go on to be joined by Buddhism in the trinity of 'teachings' which dominated Chinese thought during the imperial age. An education based on the Classics linked with the name of Confucius had been advocated by Hsün Tzu; so, as the prestige of the resurgent Confucian school grew, these books were well placed to be chosen as the curriculum for the growing bureaucracy. Hereafter a new brand of Confucianism, which had absorbed some Legalist and Taoist elements, became the official philosophy of the state. Its future dominance was assured when the centuries of division following the downfall of the Later Han Dynasty early in the third century AD coincided with a period when Buddhism had much political influence; for when unity was restored to China in the late sixth century AD it was to Confucianism (the creed of the great Han empire and the only available model of a successful ideology of imperial government) that the Sui rulers and eventually their T'ang successors naturally turned for an educational programme and a political philosophy.

The system of open examinations based on the study of ancient texts which would give students the general moral training needed by a ruling élite owed much to Confucius's own ideals and practices, such as his belief that there should be no class-distinctions in education, his use of the *Songs* in teaching, and his concept of the gentleman as a generalist and not one whose special skills might make him the implement of others. For the intellectuals of imperial China he also provided a personal example of conduct to which both student and teacher should aspire, with his lifelong commitment to learning despite poverty and discouragement, which was echoed in the life-style of his favourite disciple Yen Hui. For Confucius the purpose of learning was to fit oneself for official employment or, failing that, to teach others with the same aim in view; and this very same task was set before the scholars of imperial China. The content of learning was not the nuts and bolts of administrative practice, but the moral training aimed at producing officials whose conduct would be a model for the people to imitate and reciprocate; so self-cultivation or the cultivation of the moral personality was the heart of the matter. This concentration on self-cultivation was always to be an important feature of the ethos of the scholar-bureaucrat. It deeply affected his attitudes to cultural activities such as painting and writing poetry, which often seemed to be viewed primarily as exercises in self-cultivation.

In considering the subject-matter of education we became aware of the supreme importance attached to the handing on of tradition. Confucius himself claimed to be a transmitter and not a creator, entrusted with the task of handing down traditions about the Golden Age of the early Chou Dynasty. His essential message was that harmony could be restored by imitating the Way of an ideal past. The books in which the deeds of the ancients were recorded were consequently destined to be at the forefront of education and culture, and Chinese society became imbued with a powerful traditionalism in which the primary concern of scholarship was the preservation and interpretation of the ancient literature. This traditionalism inevitably resulted in a high degree of cultural unity. Despite the great regional diversity of China and the numerous distinct local cultures, the intellectuals were dominated by a 'great tradition' based on this single orthodoxy. At the same time it was culture which distinguished the Chinese from barbarians, and it was a cultural rather than a racial unity which had its embodiment in the Chinese state. Everyone could and would become Chinese. The Classics associated with Confucius were not the property of a single sect. The Confucian literature was the heritage of the whole people. The language in which this literature was written was kept artificially alive as the appropriate medium for all serious writing, a further powerful promoter of cultural unity and traditionalism. The script also played its part: like numerals, which are universally intelligible to the eye although pronounced differently in different languages, Chinese characters provided a common means of communication which united people even if they spoke mutually unintelligible dialects. But the inspiration for cultural unity and traditionalism may be clearly seen in words attributed to Confucius.

An important feature of the cultural unity inspired by the Confucian writings was the role of *li* (ritual), the rules of which, as we have seen, were thought of, not as the mores of a particular society, but as a universally valid system. Similarly the filial piety associated with the name of Confucius was universalised in the *Book of Filial Piety* and regarded as a cosmic principle. The ancient Confucian literature regarded the family as the microcosm of the state, so that the essence of government was to provide an example of adherence to family virtues for the people to follow and reciprocate in the form of loyalty. This image was preserved in imperial China and utilised by governments which saw the family and clan as convenient implements of political control. If the clans stressed the family virtues and thus secured order among their own members, they were doing the government's job for it. In a society in which order was ideally preserved by the constraints of ritual and the family virtues, the use of law was, as Confucius had suggested, a confession of failure; but in the real world there had to be a legal system. However, such was the domination of the Confucian ethos that not only were penalties graded in accordance with the pattern of family obligations, but also the law reflected the class distinction between the gentleman, for whom the obligations of ritual made it strictly speaking unnecessary, and the small man, who needed to be controlled by fear of punishments. Confucius's contrast between the gentleman motivated by justice and the small man motivated by profit was also reflected in the class system in imperial China, which placed the scholars on top and the merchants at the bottom. The ruling élite, as Confucius would have wished, was increasingly recruited on the basis of intellectual and ethical qualifications rather than birth. The imperial role was also in theory based on the ancient ideal of the benevolent ruler entrusted with the Mandate of Heaven, whose manifestation of exemplary virtue brings tranquillity to his own people and wins over the barbarians.

We have seen that the sayings attributed to Confucius have had a profound influence on educational, social, and political ideals and practices in China. If we turn now to literature and art, we shall see that the Confucian influence also permeates these areas of the Chinese experience. We have already noticed the pre-eminent position among the categories of literature which had been assigned to the Classics ever since Hsün Tzu stressed their educational value. We have seen that historical writing is imbued with such Confucian ideals as the provision of model characters for emulation or avoidance, as well as the belief that the recording of virtuous deeds brings lasting glory to one's ancestors. We have noticed that Confucius's use of the *Songs* sets the pattern for the utilisation of literature for the purpose of moral training; while novels and short stories have been disesteemed for not being vehicles for the dissemination of the orthodox Confucian morality.

Art is generally considered an area in which Taoism and Buddhism have more to say than Confucianism, but Confucian scholar-officials were the main arbiters of taste and the largest body of art patrons the world has ever known. The work of the scholar-painters, who were at the forefront of the Chinese artistic tradition, was naturally imbued with Confucian ideals. The business of painting, like the writing of poetry, was conceived as part of the regime of self-cultivation; and the resultant works always conformed with the Confucian sense of propriety and harmony. The demands of *li* were imperative in art as in social life. Chinese paintings did not show scenes of horror or violence. Art had educational value since it reflected the self-cultivation of the Confucian gentleman. The contemplation of portraits of exemplary figures from the past was as morally inspiring as reading their biographies in the dynastic histories; and another edifying *genre* was the illustration of morally enlightening episodes from life or literature. Landscape paintings too were full of a Confucian tranquillity and decorum, merging with the Taoist concept of man's communion with that nature of which he was himself a part.

Because of the agnostic sayings attributed to him Confucius is sometimes thought not to have had much influence on the religious lives of the Chinese people, especially in view of the powerful influence of Buddhism and other creeds. But the *Record of Rites*, which features Confucius as an expert on ritual, did provide detailed instructions for marriages, funerals, ancestor worship, and for the celebration of other important religious occasions; and in imperial China scholars played important parts in religious ceremonies because of their command of this literature. It should also be remembered that Confucius himself was worshipped as a god. He had rejected the lesser honour of sagehood and would have been horrified at this development; but he was so venerated in the Later Han Dynasty that regular worship of him was conducted in government schools, and in the

T'ang Dynasty temples to the Master were erected throughout the empire. In these temples the chief disciples and distinguished Confucians of later ages were also honoured. Above the altar were the words 'The teacher of ten thousand generations', and only scholars could take part in the sacrifices. As the patron deity of scholars and officials Confucius became an important figure in the state pantheon. In this capacity his role was somewhat comparable with that of the patron deities of the various crafts, which were communally worshipped by practitioners of those crafts at their guild meetings. But the supreme craft was scholarship. Confucius owes his supremacy in Chinese eyes to the fact that this deeply education-conscious people regarded him as the patron and model for the whole scholar-bureaucrat class.

So much for Confucius's influence on traditional China. How has his reputation fared in the modern world? His image was bound to crumble as the atmosphere became polluted by foreign ideas. A doctrine which embraced all under Heaven could not survive China's acknowledgement of the existence of a world split into separate nation states. In the early twentieth century attempts were made to use the Master's teachings to develop a home-grown ethical system for the new China; but in the country's reduced circumstances this could not really work. Moreover, in the eyes of the revolutionary spirits who wanted to switch off the past and turn on the future it was 'Confucius and Co.' who were responsible for the humiliations of the Chinese present. It was Confucius who was to blame for the rigid and hierarchical society of the past: when the young wanted to assert themselves, they pointed the finger of scorn at the Confucian subordination of children to their parents; when women's rights were at issue, reformers could blame Confucian literature for the fact that the traditional female role was first and foremost to bear children for the perpetuation of the family line so as to ensure the continuity of ancestor-worship, which many now regarded with increasing scepticism. Those who marvelled at the wonders of Western science and technology and saw that China was helpless against the military strength of Western

nations could blame Confucius's opposition to specialisation
and deplore past concentration on the Confucian Classics to the
detriment of study of the external world. They could, for example, observe how the development of surgery had been hindered
by the doctrine of filial piety, which refused to allow the body
to be tampered with since it was a precious gift received from
one's parents. The ancient criticisms of Confucius as a pedlar of
ritual and a trickster who duped rulers with his moralistic nonsense resurfaced in the work of leading twentieth-century
writers.

On the other hand there have also been those who have regarded Confucius as a progressive figure in his own age, believing
that his emphasis on the importance of the people and his willingness to train prospective officials from whatever social back-
ground did much to undermine the old aristocratic predomi-
nance. This attitude to Confucius's historical role was still alive
in the early years of the People's Republic. But eventually im-
patience at the difficulty of rooting out the deeply implanted
conservatism of Chinese society led to Confucius being pilloried
again during the Great Proletarian Cultural Revolution. After
the downfall of the Gang of Four figurines of the Master went
on sale again in China, but in the world of the late twentieth
century one has to look for evidence of the influence of Confucian thought in a diffused form rather than as an established
and formally recognised doctrine.

Among the overseas Chinese the legacy of Confucianism may
be observed most clearly in a strong sense of family unity. On
mainland China, too, many echoes of Confucianism have continued to reverberate during the past three decades. Early communist writers consciously assimilated their ideas to familiar
philosophical themes from the native tradition, just as many
centuries earlier the foreign religion of Buddhism had been
assimilated to native Chinese doctrines. The communist idea of
remoulding the personality to acquire the correct proletarian
class attitudes is far from alien to a people used to the Confucian
emphasis on self-cultivation and moulding of the personality as
the basis for moral and political life. A strict orthodoxy based on

the Confucian Classics has its modern counterpart in the adoption of the sayings and writings of Chairman Mao as the repository of truth. Very traditional, too, is the use of exemplars in political education; for model workers, model communes and model industrial enterprises remind us that traditional Chinese education laid great stress on the imitation of models. Traditional and modern China have also shared a preference for political correctness to the detriment of technical expertise. Just as Confucius disparaged specialisation and the imperial civil service consequently favoured generalists schooled in the ethico-political orthodoxy, so until recently the party line has generally held that it is more important to be 'red' than 'expert', since nothing worthwhile can be achieved except on the basis of right thinking.

So the Confucian tradition is still far from dead. What I have written about him has much to do with the impact of the myth rather than the man, but despite the caution and scepticism it is necessary to bring to such an investigation, in reading the *Analects* we seem to be in touch with a real personality, not just an anthology of sayings. We seem to get glimpses of what Confucius was really like. His own distillation of a lifetime's experience is a highly personal account of his moral development: 'At fifteen I set my heart on learning, at thirty I was established, at forty I had no perplexities, at fifty I understood the decrees of Heaven, at sixty my ear obeyed them, and at seventy I could follow what my heart desired without transgressing what was right' (A 2.4). This account of self-cultivation and of the internalisation of moral imperatives seems remarkably consistent with the message of his teaching. Many of his qualities have an endearing familiarity: on his death bed he showed a typical hostility to sham; for, when his disciples dressed up as official retainers to enhance the dignity of his passing, he reproved them, saying that he would rather die in the arms of disciples than underlings (A 9.11). Indeed it is his relationships with his disciples, his different reactions to the studious Yen Hui and the extrovert Tzu-lu and others, which have the clearest ring of truth and seem to argue for the genuineness of the portrait which can be derived from a judicious selection of the material. The glimpses of personal life, the frugality and devotion to learning and sense of mission, accord so well with the teachings attributed to the man that one is left with a sense of unity of man and message which suggests that there might be more of the original Confucius surviving to us than cautious scholarship would permit us to believe.

I have presented the story of how his image inspired an alien society, but that is not to say that his message is entirely without universal appeal. Some of the sayings could profitably be adopted by anyone as mottoes, such as 'I am not worried about not being appointed; I am concerned about how I may fit myself for appointment. I am not worried that nobody knows me; I seek to become fit to be known' (A 4.14). His major concern, too, was a universal one – that political power should be wielded by men of wisdom and virtue. This was also Plato's ideal, and it remains the greatest anxiety of our world today. And his message to the individual also transcends cultural and racial differences: it is that one should strive for humaneness, seeking to cultivate the moral qualities within one so that one fully realises one's humanity.

Perhaps the most remarkable feature of the Confucian moulding of Chinese civilisation was that the sage and his disciples did not achieve this by introducing sophisticated new concepts such as justice, liberty, or democracy, which have elsewhere been valued as the hallmarks of civilised society. On the contrary they may be seen as bringing to completion the process whereby basic animal instincts developed into the guidelines of a great civilisation. Their concept of education developed out of the basic instinct of the young to imitate their elders. The family virtues derived from the basic instinct of family collaboration for survival. *Jen* (humaneness) was a sublimation of the fundamental need of human beings to collaborate for the sake of their own self-interest. And *li* (ritual) was founded on the desire of primitive man to try to gain control over his environment by means of magic. Confucianism shows how basic animal instincts can be transformed into the stuff of high civilisation by means of self-cultivation within society.

At the heart of Confucianism there was a rare humanism and a cry for mankind to be guided by moral considerations, which could not long survive in its purest form in this imperfect world. The Confucian message was adapted by politicians to suit the needs of an autocratic state, although the Master's original vision was preserved in the hearts of many individuals. Despite the distortions that his doctrine suffered during the imperial age, no human being has ever shaped his country's civilisation more thoroughly than Confucius. No human being has been set up as an example to more of his fellow human beings than Confucius. The stature which he already enjoyed more than two thousand years ago is summed up in Ssu-ma Ch'ien's biography. Since the main purpose of this book has been to explain Confucius's impact on his own people, the final assessment of him by his country's greatest historian may provide a fitting conclusion:

The world has seen many men, from kings down to ordinary men of talent and virtue, who have found glory during their lives which has come to an end with their deaths. But Confucius, although he wore the cotton gown of a commoner, has maintained his reputation for more than ten generations, and men of learning exalt him. From the Son of Heaven and the princes and nobles downwards, all those in the Middle Kingdom who speak of the six arts are guided and corrected by the Master, and this may be regarded as perfect sagehood.

Sources and further reading

While writing this book I have been very conscious that I have had space to mention only a relatively small proportion of the sayings of Confucius. The translations of the *Analects* most commonly referred to are J. Legge, *The Chinese Classics*, vol. 1 (reprinted by Hong Kong University Press, 1961) and A. Waley, *The Analects of Confucius* (Allen and Unwin, London, 1938). Although heavily Victorian in tone, the former is still a useful reference, with text, translation, and comment; and Waley's stylish translation has a useful introduction which has stood the test of time quite well. Waley's work stratifies the *Analects*, but the very recently published version by D. C. Lau (Penguin Books, Harmondsworth, 1979) treats the text as a unity. It has an introduction which contains a valuable exposition of Confucius's moral philosophy. A large number of chapters are also translated, with introductory material, in E. R. Hughes, *Chinese Philosophy in Classical Times* (Dent, London, 1942), W. T. Chan, *A Source Book in Chinese Philosophy* (Princeton University Press, 1963) and W. T. de Bary, ed., *Sources of Chinese Tradition* (Columbia University Press, New York, 1960).

These three volumes also include material on other works of the ancient Confucian school, notably *Mencius*, the best translation of which is D. C. Lau's *Mencius* (Penguin Books, Harmondsworth, 1970), and *Hsün Tzu*, on whom see B. Watson, *Hsün Tzu: Basic Writings* (Columbia University Press, New York, 1963). Another translation of early Confucian material is E. R. Hughes, *The Great Learning and the Mean in Action* (Dent, London, 1942), and the *Record of Rites* is translated by J. Legge in books 27–8 of M. Müller, ed., *Sacred Books of the East* (Clarendon Press, Oxford, 1879–1910). Ssu-ma Ch'ien's biography of Confucius is translated by Lin Yutang in *The Wisdom of Confucius* (Modern Library, New York, 1938). Other books on ancient Chinese philosophy which contain valuable material on Confucianism are D. Munro, *The Concept of Man in Early China* (Stanford University Press, 1969) and K. C. Hsiao, *A History of Chinese Political Thought*, vol. 1 (Princeton University Press, 1979). H. G. Creel's *Confucius, the Man and the Myth* (John Day, New York, 1949) is an imaginative but occasionally over-popularised account by a distinguished scholar. D. H. Smith's *Confucius* (Temple Smith, London, 1973) is by a former missionary. Both these books devote much space to the history of Confucianism after the Master's death. J. Ching, *Confucianism and Christianity* (Kodansha International, Tokyo, 1977) is a recent comparative study. On Confucius as a god the standard work is J. K. Shryock, *The Origin and Development of the State Cult of Confucianism* (Century, New York, 1932); and C. K. Yang's *Religion in Chinese Society* (University of California Press, Berkeley and Los Angeles, 1961) contains some excellent material on the religious aspects of Confucianism. Other general works about later Confucianism which can be consulted with much profit are D. S. Nivison and A. F. Wright, eds., *Confucianism in Action* (Stanford University Press, 1959) and A. F. Wright, ed., *The Confucian Persuasion* (Stanford University Press, 1960).

Index

References to the *Analects*